Tagore's
Dance-Drama Omnibus

Tagore's Dance-Drama Omnibus

Translated & Introduced by

UTPAL K BANERJEE

NIYOGI BOOKS

Published by

NIYOGI BOOKS

D-78, Okhla Industrial Area, Phase-I
New Delhi-110 020, INDIA
Tel: 91-11-26816301, 49327000
Fax: 91-11-26810483, 26813830
email: niyogibooks@gmail.com
website: www.niyogibooks.com

Design: Shashi Bhushan Prasad/Niyogi Books

ISBN: 978-93-81523-53-7

Photo Courtesy:
1. Photographs of Shadhona, Bangladesh: Smt. Lubna Mariam.
2. Photographs of Dakshinee, UK: Dr. Ananda Gupta.
3. Photographs of Pallavi, Bangladesh: Sh. Pankaj Kumar
4. Photographs of Darpana: Smt. Mrinalini Sarabhai.

Publication: 2013

Printed at: Niyogi Offset Pvt. Ltd., New Delhi, India

Smt. Mrinalini Sarabhai
only living dance-disciple
of
Rabindranath Tagore

Contents

Fireflies, Shadhona, Dhaka, Bangladesh. Photo: Ridwan Adid Rupon.

pg 2-3: Firefiles based on Tagore's poems. Shadhona, Dhaka, Bangladesh; Photo: Ridwan Adid Rupon.

Front Cover: Shapmochan, Pallavi, Dhaka, Bangladesh; Photo: Pankaj Kumar.

Introduction

The six dance-dramas translated in this book camouflage a crowning touch of Rabindranath Tagore's dance-interest in its most effulgent manifestation. It was only in the last half decade of Tagore's life that his dance-consciousness reached its zenith and he could offer the best of his life-time passion for dance in the form of six dance-dramas, namely, two music-dramas: *Tasher Desh* (interspersed with prose dialogue), *Shapmochan* (with narration), and four full-bodied dance-dramas: *Chitrangada*, *Shyama*, *Chandalika* and *Mayar Khela* (re-visited). The thematic features of these six dance-dramas have been summarised below. All the dance-dramas were, in a sense, akin to the earlier *Valmiki Pratibha* and *Kalmrigaya*, predominantly 'recitative' music dramas. The clear story-line was piggybacked mainly on the 'recitative' pattern of the melodiously articulated dialogues and narratives, interlaced with songs.

Even though Tagore's dance-dramas were meant to be enacted in the form of dance, the main *rasa* of each play was to be kept uppermost in mind. The dancers were vehicles of conveying that spirit to the viewers, dwarfing their individual skills and dexterity all the while. The male and female dancers often came from the background of different styles and techniques. But the aim defined for them by Tagore was to convey correctly the nuances of the song they were meant to dance with.

*

In order to provide fully-poetic translation of these dance-dramas—as per the flavour of the original—the idea has been to proffer the global English-speaking readership some glimpses into the poetical metre of Tagore's original writing in Bengali language. The translation-format has been as follows:

- The original rhyme-scheme of the relevant lyrics has been closely followed in English—as far as possible—with the original's rhythmic resonance to emerge;
- Both in text and in lyrics, the Poet's use of *antarmil* (internal rhyme) has been carefully kept in view, with—wherever possible—demarcations of upper case;
- The original libretto's metre, as determined by the number and length of 'feet' in Tagore's lines has been as scrupulously followed as possible;
- Translator's creative freedom, unavoidable in sticking to the original textual flavour and lyrical rhyme has been guardedly kept to the minimum, and as close to the original's meaning as possible. Such minimal poetic licence will be hopefully forgiven by the perceptive reader. In any case, qualitatively and quantitatively, they will be found far less than the self-confessed 'transmogrifications' by Edward Fitzgerald (1809-1883) in rendering his world-famous *Rubayyat of Omar Khayyam* (first published in 1858). Khayyam's all the original *dohas* (couplets) were, in translation, made into *chaupais* Quatrains), to start with!
- To note that three choral Palī hymns used by Tagore in *Chandalika* and one Sanskrit hymn used in duet at *Chitrangada's* end have been retained in original.

Tasher Desh

Tagore described *Tasher Desh* as: 'romance and realism put side by side'. Arising out of a short story *Ektà Ashade Galpa* (A Cock-and-Bull Story), at the suggestion of Pratima Devi, it took the form of a full prose-drama in a very short time. Created in 1933, the play was hugely successful, enacted in six years on nine occasions—in Calcutta, Bombay and Santiniketan—till 1939, within Tagore's own lifetime, and underwent many changes on each occasion except for the last one.

In essence, *Tasher Desh* is an out-and-out fantasy, with two sets of characters: the Prince and his travel companion on one side and the minions of the Card Kingdom—club, spade, heart and diamond, culled from the card-game—masquerading in mobile human forms, on the other side. The setting is the Card Kingdom itself, where the Prince lands after a shipwreck and takes the humanoid Cards by surprise. The rousing conflict is between the wayward, happy-go-lucky Prince with this group and the stodgy, rule-bound Cards: their two worlds being poles apart. The plot thickens when the Card-women begin breaking rules and the precipice of the Card Kingdom—with its age-old pinnacles of ossified rituals and built-in prejudices—falls by the wayside. The play is from the point of view of the freedom-loving Prince who eventually 'contaminates' the whole Kingdom, even the King, and the tone throughout remains one of biting irony. The mood, therefore, is entirely iconoclastic!

Tasher Desh was, on balance, an emphatic statement of Tagore that no social system could carry on indefinitely by basing itself on a web of soulless, meaningless set of regulations. And no such superstructure of rules and rituals, imposed on society by the powers-that-be, could be everlasting; it is bound to crumble down one day at the flimsiest of resistance. The Prince was able to remove the cobwebs of the Cards Kingdom not through war or through muscle-power or even through craftiness, but simply through the open defiance by the female populace—itself a first—through an abounding message of joy and infectious fearlessness that touched one and all, even the Card King!

Shapmochan

Shapmochan, rightly speaking, is a musical narrative where the powerful storyline, which is recited by a narrator, is interspersed with songs and mime-action, most of which are integrally interwoven with dance. The occasion was the observation of the Poet's seventieth birthday in 1931 when Tagore wrote out the narrative in running prose, based on *Raja* (1911) and *Arup Ratan* (1920), for enactment on 'Students Day' in Calcutta.

Thematically, Tagore ascribed the genesis of *Shapmochan* to the Buddhist *Kush Jataka* where the legend has a Bodhisattva born as an utterly ugly-looking king, Kush, who is married at his mother's behest to the beauteous princess of Madra Desh. The marriage, consummated only in total darkness to hide the king's ugly visage, falls apart and the dissatisfied princess then returns home. After many dramatic vicissitudes, Kush becomes a handsome prince, blessed by the jewel *Virochan* (name of another Bodhisattva) and the couple re-unites in happiness. Neither *Raja* nor *Arup Ratan* the earlier versions explains the genesis of the king's ugly countenance, but in *Shapmochan's* overture, Tagore does mention an incident of the king's previous life in paradise when he was a singing *gandharva* in the royal court of Indra where, having made a serious mistake in his music concert, he was cursed by the latter to be born on earth.

Characters in *Shapmochan* are few and far between. After the overture in Indra's court—with king Indra, queen Sachi, *gandharva* Sourasen and *gandharvi* Madhushri—leading to the curse as *cause celeb*, the rest of the narrative features only the utterly lonely earthling-queen Kamalika (besides her occasional maids) and her pining lover-king Aruneshvar (with companion). The latter remains hidden from her presence throughout the play. The setting is a fantasy-space purported to be the boudoir of the queen. The conflict is entirely in Kamalika's domain, who is constantly beseeching Aruneshvar's visible presence as well as lamenting the unfairness of his 'willful' invisibility. The narrator switches the points of view from one protagonist to the other. The tone is quite lyrical and the mood verges on the spiritual: between the ardent devotee and her besought godhead. Indeed, the burning passion of the queen for her desired 'vision' could be rubbed off on the Sufiana *kalam* of the distant Persian shores. This was perhaps nearest to Sufism from another ethos—moving from mundane love of *ishq majazi* (where both lovers endure normal earthly feelings of joy and pain, agony and ecstasy) to ethereal love of *ishq haqqiqi* (where the lover is a human being and the beloved is God).

Chitrangada

Tagore wrote his major poetic work *Chitrangada* in 1892, as a verse-play taking the original characters from the epic Mahabharata. Written in blank verse and divided into eleven sections, the verse-play recounts, in flashback, how Princess Chitrangada—brought up in the garb of a boy by her father, the king of Manipur—was rejected by the Pandava-hero Arjuna and how she seeks from the God of Love supreme feminine beauty to conquer Arjuna. The boon is granted and the new Chitrangada is able to lure Arjuna, notwithstanding his vows as a hermit, and spends a year in conjugal bliss. Every good thing has to come to an end, for Arjuna wakes up to reclaim his masculine prowess and encounter bandits in Manipur, an act accomplished earlier by Princess Chitrangada. The veil falls and the princess meets her lover now: as an equal and without any pretence. The play's slightly abridged nine-act version, *Chitra*, appeared in 1914, in Tagore's own English translation.

Already well structured as verse-play, *Chitrangada*, first enacted in 1936 as a dance-drama in Calcutta, is still tauter in its six-act depiction: with dramatic events played out without flashback and with the character Vasanta dropped altogether. There are only three major characters: Chitrangada (with female companions), Arjuna and *Madana* (God of Love). The setting is mainly the Manipur forests and the hermitage of the recluse Arjuna. The see-saw conflict is very real: 'early' Chitrangada's overture to Arjuna and the latter's stern rejection; 'new' Chitrangada's reluctant offer of the self and Arjuna's instant surrender of male machismo; Chitrangada's constant self-introspection and Arjuna's conjugal fervour; and so on, till the resolution of conflict takes place on equal terms. The point of view is mainly Chitrangada's, with Arjuna's egotistic self-opinion playing only a second fiddle. The tone is of self-examination throughout for Chitrangada whose mood is wildly variant spanning: utter dejection; earnest devotion; veiled jubilation; conjugal elation; jaded satiation; and final self-revelation on equal terms.

Beyond the riddance of individual infatuation at the tortuous end, there is a higher dimension: about femininity. The 1892 verse-play began on the note of an abject offer of surrendering of womanhood to the altar of man, to be his companion, charioteer, follower in hunting, night-guard, devotee, servant and subject—while the 1936 dance-drama catapults the image to a transcendental level, in Tagore's own words: 'I am Chitra. No goddess to be worshipped, nor yet the object of common pity to be brushed aside like a moth with indifference. If you deign to keep me by your side in the path of danger and daring, if you allow me to share the great duties of your life, then you will know my true self'. This is the triumphant voice of universal femininity! Indeed, Tagore was very particular about the stentorian proclamation of the princess in the finale: 'I'm Chitrangada, the daughter of the king of kings; I'm neither a goddess nor an ordinary female'. He urged the protagonist: 'Never forget your exalted status; express it to the hilt in all your feelings and gestures'. This was mood dance of the rejoicing womanhood!

Shyama

Like *Chitrangada*, *Shyama* underwent many versions. Inspired originally by the Buddhist story from *Mahavastu Avadan*, the first version was *Parishodh*, a long episodic poem written in 1899, about the royal courtesan Shyama and her sudden passion for the handsome stranger Vajrasen—caught on a false charge of theft—for whom she does not hesitate to sacrifice her young lover Uttiyo at the gallows. On the felony being known, she is summarily discarded by her 'new' lover Vajrasen. In the rhymed poem, the rich resonance of Nature—to the variegated course of raw passion and its retribution—is unparalleled, a role taken up by Shyama's female companions as the 'voice of conscience', in what Tagore called 'dramatised musical' version of *Parishodh* in 1938. The musical note was set entirely in melody and, unlike *Chitrangada*; no portion was left for simple oral narration. *Shyama* was the final version, substantially enlarged and enriched, enacted as dance-drama at Santiniketan and Calcutta, in 1938 and 1939.

The two main protagonists are Shyama and Vajrasen, besides the king's minions as well as the youth Uttiyo, with the courtesan's companions acting as a 'voice of conscience' and serving the same purpose as they did for Princess Chitrangada in the eponymous play—a well-known ploy used in Bengali folk-drama *Jatra* essayed by *Vivek*, literally meaning conscience. The setting varies from a public avenue, to Shyama's chambers, to the prison-cell, to the luxury-yacht carrying the fleeing lover-duo, to the forests on the riverbank, to the final separation. The plot is playing out of *amour propre* between the lovers: now infatuated, now quarrelling and desperately estranged. The point of view is entirely Shyama's: besotted with passion and eager to elope, to the admission of her felony and her eventual desertion. The mood is of the urgency of the lovers' union: only to fall apart. The tone is, for both lovers, psychologically nuanced—unlike the deep intelligence and understanding of Chitrangada, countered by a strident Arjuna, deliberately vaunting bravado of male ego. The primary beauty of *Shyama* is the heaving rise and fall of its conflicts and their Spenserian tempo: almost like the Western music's overture with *allegro*, leading on to *adagio* and *rondo*, and then to the denouement in *adagio*: on the waxing and waning of the passage of arduous passion between the two principal contenders.

The import of *Shyama* is in the overwhelming guilt, which Shyama carries that makes her unacceptable to Vajrasen. The heinous depth of Shyama's guilt for making the innocent Uttiyo a victim of her 'lust' for Vajrasen—all the more galling because Uttiyo is far too young and still willingly offers his life—makes it comparable to the Christian Guilt: with Shyama as the sinning *femme fatale* and Vajrasen as the condemning Lord, and with the same overtones of temptation and manipulation. Vajrasen seems to be both cursing and be cursed: first at his outburst of love and then at the wretchedness of his situation of having been saved from sure death at such an enormous cost. The other and more material messages are equally relevant, such as, the foreigner being duped, the need to keep the administration well-oiled at any expense, the power of money to the minions of the establishment, the reach of wealth ('royal ring') even into the dungeons and the fatal attraction of sexual favours apparent everywhere. These messages are valid to this day.

Chandalika

Chandalika, like the other two dance-dramas, had a chequered history. It was written first, in 1933, as a two-act prose-play and adapted from *Shardula-Karna Avadana*, a part of the Nepali Buddhist lore, and confined virtually to a dialogue between Prakriti and her mother. The story, as encapsulated by Tagore, takes place at Shravasti where the Buddha is residing temporarily. His favourite disciple Ananda, once after a meal with a householder, feels thirsty while returning and asks for drinking water from Prakriti, a *chandali*, who was fetching water from the well-side. Prakriti gets infatuated with the handsome monk and, in the absence of any other alternative, seeks help from her mother who knew magic. The mother, initially reluctant, performs her elaborate magic rites and throws one hundred and eight *arka* flowers, one by one, into the sacrificial fire. Ananda is unable to resist the magical force and arrives at her place in the night. While Prakriti is preparing the nuptial bed, Ananda feels severe compunction and prays fervently with tears to the Buddha for redemption. The distant savant realises the condition of his devotee and rescues him from the mantras of the *chandali*.

Tagore was acutely aware of the countrywide spread of communal disharmony and was deeply pained about its evil consequences. He turned the play into a 'recitative' form and after adding a few songs from his available repertoire innovated with a number of brand new prose lyrics and set them to music. Lyrical prose, incidentally, did not occur in any other dance-drama earlier. The play was staged in Calcutta and at Santiniketan in 1938 and 1939. The 1940 performance at Santiniketan was witnessed by Mahatma Gandhi and was highly appreciated by him for its theme of untouchability.

The much enlarged three-act *Chandalika* has many characters, besides Prakriti and her mother, such as the upper-caste village-belles who take quite a dim view of Prakriti's efforts to hobnob with the flower-vendors, curd-seller and bangle-supplier. There are also chanting *Shamans* and their leader Ananda. The setting is the milieu by the well-side and the secluded hamlet. The plot is virtually the same as the Buddhist episode, barring that the latter's innuendos of physical union are wonderfully sublimated into deeply divisive psychological conflicts—starting with the mother's mind—from simplistic caste reservations to a fiendish proclivity to wield witchcraft and ending with Ananda's transcendental purity torn asunder under the spell of magic and the unbearable pain of potential perdition.

But the utmost conflict is within Prakriti: between her passionate love and carnal desire for Ananda on one hand, and the convulsions in her mind on the other—by realising the monk's anguish, not merely to let him free but also to fall into his footsteps: a substantial departure from the original ending. The point of view is primarily that of Prakriti: a mindset that changes from muted acceptance of social rejection to an awakening into 'spiritual freedom' in this birth itself (enunciated remarkably well in the Buddhist *Lotus Sutra*), from her fiercely possessive passion for Ananda to an enlightenment to follow him, which is normally much above her station of life. The mood is largely of desperation to achieve a self-defined goal and the tone varies from a stentorian call to her mother to get to the desired object fast up to the shearing self-flagellation that tears her into total submissiveness. Conflicts in *Chandalika*—both inter-character as well as intra-character—are on an extraordinarily large scale. Also, each conflict spans a wide range: rising to a precipice and diving down to a deep gorge: almost staccato in nature. If Tagore took liberty in using prose-librettos to express a gritty, earthy texture in his text, he did justice to their variety and range by using an incredible diversity of tunes.

The play bears three clear messages. At the very outset, it is a low-caste struggle for survival, humiliating and infra-dig at every moment of its existence, from which the symbolic act of offering water to the monk provides a redemption, a birth into new human dignity: never experienced before, something that appealed to the Mahatma and attracted generations of dancers ever since. At another level, it is a primordial tussle between lust and love, between passion and its resolution, beginning in the warp and weft of Prakriti's humdrum life and ending in her devout surrender to the profundity of new values that Ananda revealed to her. But if that is true for Prakriti, it is also an upheaval within Ananda's mind, as seen in the magic mirror and in the shadow play. He is torn between the protection of his wisdom as well as the attraction of the mortal world to its carnal desires. It is eventually a triumph of the higher values that allow the power of his spirit to rise above the sensuality of the flesh. But at a spiritual level, it is a metaphor of the eternal duel between *Purusha* and *Prakriti*, the dormant force and the driving power—the confrontation between the *Yin* and the *Yang*—that drives the entire material universe.

Mayar Khela

Written within a decade of Tagore's return from England, his *Mayar Khela* (1888) was similar to a pre-Wagner opera of the West: dominated by songs with very little dramatic outline. Tagore himself termed it: 'a musical outpouring when the mind was entirely drenched with melody'. When re-visited, it was called 'dance-drama' by Tagore, at the behest of Pratima Devi, his daughter-in-law and was proposed by her for dance *abhinaya*, in 1938–39. The script was tightened to two-third of its earlier length and as many as sixteen new songs were added, although male and female characters were not really altered. Tagore explained the alterations thus: I had only attempted to express mental feelings at my early age, which I hope I have undone now. The feelings at a mature age are not to be merely verbalised in songs, but are to be viewed essentially for their beauty.

Both these versions are fantasy games of love and separation, not materially different from each other. Each has two female protagonists—Pramada and Shanta—besides the illusive maidens or *maya kumaris* and the trio of male characters, out of whom Amar is sought after, Kumar is the roaming Casanova and Ashok is the eternal lover. The setting is an illusive forest. The conflicts are forever effervescent: now uniting, now separating and now consummating again, to all of which the maidens are alternately stoking fires of desire and despair. There are no specific points of view, except that of passion: unquenched or satiated. The tone and the mood are vaguely reminiscent of Shakespeare's *A Midsummer Night's Dream*: both set in fantasy woods like a dreamland; with shades of Shakespeare's Titania, Queen of the Fairies, evident in Tagore's Pramada and Shanta; Fairies and their repetitive solos and choruses resembling the recursive musical refrains of the illusive maidens; the love-potion in sleep akin to Amar's sudden drowsiness; and the attitude of the Fairies to mortals much similar to the illusive maidens' mindset for the three hapless males. Only Puck and his Puckish humour, if anything, is missing in the later poet's work!

*

A detailed introspection on the background of all the six dance-dramas and an in-depth analysis of their choreographic and other aesthetic features will be found in the author's companion-volume, *Tagore's Mystique of Dance,* brought out by the same publishers in 2011.

Tasher Desh

(Kingdom of Cards)

Fast wind swiftly glides,
Clouds spread on all sides,
O oarsman, your boat you row,
Tightly you do steer,
I set sail'n'bind here—
Haul by rope, haul by rope, heave ho!

On chains oft is jingling clatter,
It's not boat's worried wailing matter–
Turbulent bonds are beyond all chatter: they're all tumbling, much so:
Haul by rope, haul by rope, heave ho!

Counting day'n'time,
Agitating mind's chimes,
Don't say 'To go or not to go',
The sea of anxiety
Cross in mental piety,
Don't look out ever so.

If eternity does overwhelm,
matted hairs wayward stem, Storms do plunder,
waves huge heights claim,
Don't cower under, strike rhythms the same—let victory-song flow:
Haul by rope, haul by rope, heave ho!

Scene One

The prince and the merchant are present.

Prince: It can't really go on any more, friend!

Merchant: Why are you restless, Prince?

Prince: How can I explain? Tell me what the restlessness is of that flock of swans which, in spring, fly in droves towards the Himalayas.

Merchant: They do have their nests there!

Prince: If the nests are there, why do they leave them at all? No, no, they enjoy the pleasure of flight, the pleasure that defies reason.

Merchant: Do you want to fly?

Prince: Of course, I do!

Merchant: I can't understand your words! I do feel it's better to be closed inside a cage with reason than to fly without reason!

Prince: Why do you say with reason?

Merchant: I stay inside the golden a cage for the temptation of food and drink.

Prince: You won't understand, you won't.

Merchant: I have that fault; I don't understand what's beyond comprehension.

Why don't you clarify a little what appears so intolerable to you?

Prince: These boring days in the palace!

Merchant: Do you call it boring? There's so much management, such paraphernalia!

Prince: I feel myself like a stone-icon in a golden temple! The conches, the bells and the bell-metal dishes are tolling

Tasher Desh, Shadhona, Dhaka, Bangladesh. Photo: KM Asad.

pg 21: Tasher Desh, Shadhona, Dhaka, Bangladesh. Photo: KM Asad.

within heard in the same monotonous sound! The ritual food-offerings remain the same, but there's no taste in the consumption! Can this be tolerated?

Merchant: It can be quite tolerated by folks like us! It's lucky that the quantum is fixed. Had it been loose, we'd collapse in desperation! Whatever we receive is enough for the hunger. And what you don't get is what you probably seek to satisfy the mental hunger!

Prince: And what about the mendicants' chants every day that you have to listen to all around in the same rhyme—that '*Shardulabikridita*'?

Merchant: I think that the more you hear chants repeatedly, the better it's for you. It never gets stale!

Prince: As soon as one wakes up, one accosts the same group of welcome-singers! And, daily morning, the same blessings are proffered by the same priest with paddy and ritual grass! And, as I come and go, I find the same old man in arms standing beside the gate like a wooden doll! If I ever step out to go somewhere, immediately the doorkeeper rushes in to ask—Here to where, here to where, here to where. All of them, put together, have suppressed the mind with verbiage.

Merchant: Why, when occasionally you go out for hunting, there's no nuisance other than the wild animals there.

Prince: Whom do you call wild animal? I gravely doubt whether the royal hunters have not put the tigers on opium! They seem to have been indoctrinated in the principle of non-violence. So far, I haven't seen any single one to leap up decently!

Merchant: Whatever you might say, I won't blame such behaviour of the tigers as anything like indecent! The organised hunting spree remains complete, the only thing taken care of are the palpitations of the heart!

Prince: The other day, I aimed at the bear from a long distance to pierce it by my arrow; everyone greatly appreciated my skill! Later, I heard whispers that a dead bear was put up stuffed in dry straw! I couldn't tolerate such sarcasm. I have ordered imprisonment of the concerned hunter.

Merchant: You've benefitted him a lot! His prison happens to be next door to the inner precincts of the Queen-mother. Only the other day, I dispatched for him three mounds of purified butter and thirty-three he-goats from our stores.

Prince: What does it all mean?

Merchant: That bear was really created at the queen-mother's command.

Prince: That's it! We're enmeshed in the web of falsehood. Our wings have got cramped inside the cage of safety. It's all make-belief: from beginning to end! They've made me into a princely sham! I feel like tearing down these royal costumes. When I find there the farmers ploughing the crop-field, I feel they must have earned virtue in their last birth to deserve being born as cultivators!

Merchant: And, pray find out as to what they think of you. Prince, you're simply talking nonsense—you're hiding the real intention in your mind. O Patralekha dear, perhaps you could guess what the secret word is in our prince's mind, why don't you ask him once?

Enters Patralekha.

Song

Patralekha:

Secret word won't remain secret.
Silent eyes have its outlet—

Prince:

No, no, no, it won't be secret.

Patralekha:

In smile bewildered
Flute's playing is heard—
In lips quivered, in dream private—

Prince:

No, no, no, it won't be secret.

Patralekha:

Hummed the honey-bee,
In sweet pain, a-thirst for light
Blossomed Ashoka tree.
Lotus-like heart
Shaking, it did start,
In purple moon, sunrays pulsate.

Prince: No, no, no, it won't be secret.

Prince: I've a secret word, that word is hidden in the far sky. I sit at the sea-shore gazing at the western horizon. There my fate has, like the proverbial miser, kept concealed something, in quest of which I shall go.

Song

I must go, I must go, dear,
I must go for trade;
I'll accost the goddess of loss,
If wealth's goddess I shade.

Merchant: What's that? Trade? You seem to be reciting the chant of a merchant!

Prince: Adorning my ship with men

Pulling oars a thousand:
Through which sea I'll journey
Reaching which far land!

Which star I shall ever aim:
Leave borders, shores disclaim,
Row boat in which direction's name
In black waves, huge—
In false hope of gold sand-beach:
I won't take refuge.

Merchant: To become missing by being the oarsman for the boundless: it doesn't seem like the route to trade! Have you received any specific news?

Prince: Haven't I? I've received gestures; I've received it in dreams!

In the blue's lap, the Blue Island
Has coral on each side,
On mountain-peaks, sea-birds have
Built nests to abide.
On branches of coconut tree
Stormy winds howl for free,
Through deep woods, have a spree
The flowing mountain-stream,
If I go there, I'll get gem of
Seven kings: of my dream.

Merchant: From the melody of your song, it is clear that this gem isn't the merchandising gem at all! Do tell me the name of this jewel please!

Prince: It's the new maiden, the new maiden!

Merchant: The new maiden? At last, a clear-cut word has been said!

Prince: It'll still take a while for it to take a clear shape.

Song

O ever-new:
On daily dust of roads I don't have your view!

The message I can hear
In spring-wind's cheer,
On first awakening, on golden cloud I see you!

Merchant: But it'd be difficult to collect the gem of this particular dream of yours!

Prince: In dream you do rest, full of fun and jest,

Which heavenly king's flower
In hair's garland you shower?
In which unknown tune, in quiet, you play veena's cue?

Enters the Queen-mother

Merchant: Queen-mother, his Lordship will like to catch the mirage in his net, he wishes to get hold of the fairyland.

Mother: What's that? Do you want to regress to childhood?

Prince: Yes, mother, my heart is panting for breath in the world surrounded by good intentions of the aged!

Mother: I've understood, dear child, your scarcity is the lack of scarcity! You've developed distaste for what's available. You had so far no chance to lack anything.

Prince:

Song

My mind says, 'I want to get, g…et, get, dear—
Me, what they won't let, dear.

In all the bequeathing
In my mind, pain is seething—
It's nowhere, for…get, forget, dear.

I'm to lose all,
For myself to re-install;

Evening star does disappear
To rise in morning star's near—
It says, 'let me s…et, s…et, set, dear.'

Mother: Child dear, I'll lose you if I attempt to hold on to you. You won't be able to bear the baggage of comfort, nor could you tolerate the bond of service. I won't invite bad luck by being scared. I'd put on the mark of white sandalwood paste on your forehead; attach a bunch of white oleanders on your crown. Let me go to offer worship to the hereditary deity of our family. In the evening, I'll apply collyrium in the eye during the prayer-greeting of the deity.

Exits the queen-mother.

Prince:

Song

Look, the sea's billowy waves
Speedily, the winds lash;
The sun goes to set there,
Lightnings in cloud splash.
I gaze at south, at north gaze,
Nothing's there, save foamy haze,
If I don't reach shore ablaze:
To bottom, I shall get,
Even then at home-corner
I won't remain upset.
Floating boat destination-less
I'm going to unknown,
In my empty boat, I'm the
Only boatman, alone.
Filling new winds in my sail
One isle to another: I'll hail,

Unforeseen gem and jewel
In my boat I'll fill—
When the beggar mind returns,
It'll be with royal thrill.

Scene Two

Prince and the merchant are present,
after a cataclysmic ship-wreck.

Prince: We began our journey from one shore, the ship sank in mid-ocean, and we've floated up on another shore. After such a long time it does appear that life are not about to begin a new chapter.

Merchant: Prince, you've always been restless about things anew. I'm scared of that very newness. Whatever you may say, the old is quite comfortable.

Prince: The frog is comfortable in the stale well. Why don't you understand, we've got out of the bottom of death. The god of death has marked our forehead with an insignia of new life.

Merchant: You've come with the royal insignia marked on your forehead at the very moment of your birth!

Prince: That's the mark of fate's giving of alms. The king of death has wiped it off with the waters of the high seas and has commanded: a new kingdom has to be conquered with new might, in a new land.—

Song

I've reached new land.
Broken boat has gone to bottom; I've reached shore's sand.

Unknown mind's rattle
I'll let hear unforeseen hope's prattle,
I'll weave sheer coloured threads' web of weal'n'woe,
In soul will new song's rhythm flow,
Wailing-laughing, I'll roam: new sorrow to understand.

Beloved, whose name I don't know
With unknown flowers' garland go
For heart-on-heart to glow.
In youth's new outburst of passion,
Fagun month's elation
Anklets in grass, will be in motion,
South wind will zoom
In clove-creeper's fresh buds' bloom,
In the waving unkempt hairs' band.

Merchant: Prince, the words seem just right in your song's tune. But let me ask: where did you find youth's fresh beauty in this land? I've been around a little. What I noticed was a bower-wood made by a carpenter! I saw that they're moving about in a square-like wooden gait; flats are fixed on the back and front; they're stepping up and down in clippety-clappety sound; it was as though they wore on feet four-cornered ankles made out of tamarind wood. Can this dead land be called a new land?

Prince: Only from this you'll realise that the thing's not real, it's artificial, it's imposed from the top, it is a slough made out by scholars of the land. What we're here for is—to remove it. When the real raw beauty will come out, it will astound all.

Merchant: We're the commercial lot; we adjudge the price from what we see with clarity. And, you've faith in what you cannot see. Well, let us see whether fire comes out of the ashes. My own feeling is that you'll lose your breath while you keep puffing. Look there, they're coming this side—it seems a ghostly dance being done by corpses!

Prince: let's go a little aside, just to watch the whole fun.

Enter the band of Cards.
Cards are marching.

Song

Push up, pull down,
Front-back, don't frown,
To left, to right,
Don't look, be uptight.
Sit, rise: never mind,
Do spread, do wind.
Topsy-turvy,
Cyclone's curve-y—
Stop, stop, stop.

Merchant: Did you see the thing? Red costume, black costume! They're rising, falling, reclining, sitting: without any rhyme or reason—how very strange! Ho, ho, ho, ho!

Six-pip Card: What's the matter: laughing?

Five-pip Card: Aren't you ashamed: laughing?

Six-pip Card: Don't you follow rules: laughing?

Prince: Laughter has at least a meaning. What you were doing has no meaning at all!

Six-pip Card: Meaning? Why do you need a meaning? What you need is the rule. Don't you understand this? Are you crazy?

Prince: It's not so easy to recognise the crazy one! How did you know?

Five-pip Card: By observing your customs and manners.

Prince: So what did you find?

Six-pip Card: We found: you've manners, but not the customs.

Merchant: And, you seem to have the customs, not manners?

Five-pip Card: Don't you know, Customs are most ancient; Manners are modern,—infantile, imbecile, immature.

Six-pip card: You haven't apparently been brought up under a proper tutor. Nobody explained to you that on the way there're pitfalls, pools of water, thorns, prickles,—manners have many handicaps!

Prince: This land obviously belongs to tutors. We'll surrender to them.

Six-pip Card: Now, what's your identification?

Prince: We're foreigners.

Five-pip Card: Stop, you won't have to say anything more. It means that you've no race, no clan, no caste, no belonging, no family, no grouping, no class, and no formation.

Tasher Desh, Shadhona, Dhaka, Bangladesh. Photo: Ridwan Adid Rupon.

Prince: No, nothing, no, nothing,—leaving everything else, what we've you can clearly see! Now, how about your identity?

Six-pip Card: We're from the world-famous Card Community. I'm Six-pip Sharman.

Five-pip Card: I'm Five-pip Varman,

Prince: And how about those who're standing away in hesitation?

Six-pip Card: That blackish one—she's Three-pip Ghosh.

Five-pip Card: And that reddish one—she's Two-pip Das.

Merchant: What's your origin?

Six-pip Card: Brahma had become exhausted in the act of creation. When he yawned in that afternoon for the first time, our genesis was from that sacred yawn.

Five-pip Card: For this reason, we're named the Yawn Community instead of the Card Community, in some heretical languages.

Merchant: How amazing!

Six-pip Card: In the sacred moment of dusk, Grandfather Brahma yawned four times simultaneously with his four faces.

Merchant: Goodness! What was the outcome?

Six-pip Card: There came out, at once, one by one—Spade, Diamond, Heart and Club. They all are worthy of salutation! *(Salutes)*

Prince: Are all of them aristocrats?

Six-pip Card: Of course, they're aristocrats! Great aristocrats, because they had an oral origin.

Five-pip Card: The most ancient poet of the Card Community, Lord Card-fun-incarnate, slept for twelve hours of the day and made out in his dream a rhyming pattern, from whose metrical steps evolved the thirty-seven thousand and a half customs of ours,

Prince: Do let us learn at least one of them.

Five-pip Card: Well, then turn you face round.

Prince: Why?

Five-pip Card: It's the rule.

Song of the band of Cards

Y-a-a-awn,
In hand, chore's gone.
Days come, days go,
Don't move to and fro.
In hand, chore's gone.

Prince: I can't bear it any longer; I have to turn my face.

Five-pip Card: Drat! You broke the spell! You made it impure!

Prince: Impure?

Five-pip Card: What else but impure? The foreigner's gaze has fallen in the middle of the chant!

Prince: What's the remedy now?

Six-pip Card: A bat-eaten mangosteen fruit-kernel has to be burnt and has to be applied as collyrium in the eyes for three days. Only then the Grandfather's fast in the heaven can be given up.

Prince: What a trouble I've caused! We've to step out very cautiously in your kingdom.

Six-pip Card: It'll be better if you don't step out at all, you'll remain pure.

Prince: What happens if one remains pure?

Five-pip Card: What could happen? You would remain pure if you are pure! Don't you understand?

Prince: It's impossible for us to understand. May I ask something,—what were you doing on that embankment in a group formation?

Six-pip Card: Fighting.

Prince: You call that fighting?

Five-pip Card: Of course, fighting in its purest of forms, in accordance with the ritual customs of the Card Community.

Tasher Desh, Shadhona, Dhaka, Bangladesh. Photo: KM Asad.

Song

We are picture, very well-dyed,
Totally pure, very sanctified!

Merchant: Let that be, but in a war there's no sap unless there's some anger and wrath.

Six-pip Card: Our anger comprises in colour.

We've battle—
No angry prattle.
See there Knave:
Soft, used to behave.

Merchant: Even then, the guns and cannons do fit well in the fighting arena.

Five-pip Card: No weapon to curb,

Just dust-hued garb.
No temptation,
No lamentation.
Not a leap,
Not to skip.

Prince: Let it not be there, but there must be some complaint! Only that can lead to fighting between two sides.

Six-pip Card:

We know usual way,
So we do obey:
Who's your enemy, who's your foe,
Who's humpty-dumpty, who's empty to go.

Five-pip Card: O foreigner dear, won't you have originated according to some scripture?

Merchant: Definitely. Right in the beginning of Creation, when Grandfather Brahma had mounted the sun on a pedestal, a fire-spark entered his nose. He sneezed making the sound of a cannon-fire,—from that earth-shaking sneeze was our genesis.

Six-pip Card: It has become clear now. That's why you're so restless.

Prince: We can't remain stable, but keep diverted in all directions.

Five-pip Card: But that's no good!

Merchant: Who said it's any good? We're still to get over the mighty push of that sneeze from the primeval times.

Six-pip Card: But I can see one good outcome—At the push of that sneeze, you'll get thrown out of this island quite early, unable to stick here.

Merchant: It'll be difficult to stay on.

Five-pip Card: Your fighting's of what kind?

Merchant: That's between the two sides on the scale of four pairs of sneezes.

Six-pip Card: On the scale of the sneeze? Goodness, won't there be then clashing of heads?

Merchant: Yes, of totally bamboozling kind!

Six-pip Card: Your ancient poet must have had a chant too?

Merchant: Of course, yes!

Song

Sneeze!
In fear, do we freeze?
To press the throat, we insist,
On face, we strike with fist,
Tell now, does comfort increase?

Six-pip Card: O dear Five-pip, they're really of the inter-caste kind! Which is your race?

Merchant: We're the Nasal race, born out of the nose.

Five-pip Card: We haven't heard of such a name for any high-caste race!

Merchant: Steam of the yawn has flown you high, beyond the other world. Force of the sneeze has struck us down below, on this side of the mundane world.

Six-pip Card: It is due to Grandfather's lack of self-control that you're so bizarre!

Prince: At last the right word has come out of your mouth. We're bizarre!

Song

We're messengers of new youth,
We're restless, we're uncouth.

Barriers we break,
Ashok wood's multi-hue passion, us, coloured do make.
Storm's bonds we rent apart—we're lightning, forsooth.

We commit mistakes—
Plunging into deep waters, for shores, fight we make.

Whenever they inform
In life-death storm, we're ready, that's truth.

Six-pip and
Five-pip Cards: *(looking at each other)* This won't go, this won't go.

Prince: We drive precisely what can't go.

Six-pack Card: But the rule?

Prince: Once the fencing breaks its rule, the road finds the rule of its own! Otherwise how can you advance?

Five-pip Card: O brother, what are they talking? They'll advance! With such a straight face, they just blurted out: they'll advance!

Prince: Why move otherwise?

Six-pip Card: Move? Why should you move? It's the rule that will move!

Song

Move as per rule.
Don't look far,
Don't make neck astir,
Go on even schedule.

Prince:

Look at forest there,
For rules, who does care?
Mad springs on south hills
Are not at all cool!

Band of Cards:

That side: don't see, don't see,
Don't go on a spree—Go on even schedule.

Five-pip Card: Talk no more, there comes King, also Lady Queen. The

Tasher Desh, Darpana, Ahmedabad, India.

Court will sit here. Now hold this branch of ground-pumpkin plant, one by one.

Prince: Branch of ground pumpkin? Ho, ho, ho, ho! Why so?

Five-pip Card: Quiet. Don't laugh. It's the rule. Look at the north-east, but never turn face to the north-west.

Six-pip Card: It's the rule.

Enter King, Queen, Ace, Knave, etc.,
with proper ritual and in customary style.

Prince: O dear brother, let's sing an adulatory chant to please the King. You please swing the ground-pumpkin branch.

Song

Victory to the progeny of Card-clan,
Surviving on fringe of sleep,
With all leisure's slain!

Band of Cards: Everything's spoilt, spoilt, spoilt! They've upset the court in inauspicious time. Ruffians!

King: Be quiet, who're they?

Six-pip Card: Foreigners.

King: Foreigners! Then the rules won't hold. Let everybody change places once, then the guilt will be taken care of. But first the national song of the Card Congregation.

All cards:

Song

Club, Spade and Heart –
In full tradition's stance
Are dancing apart
Club and Heart.
Some rise, some do fall,
Movements they do, some do stall.
Some in mirth lie on earth
To count time: stop and start.

They don't talk at all,
They don't smile,
Whoever in front comes in file:
To follow him, is their call.
Frozen is system old,
Not allowing any change bold,
No upsetting apple-cart.

King: O foreigner!

Prince: What's it, King?

King:	Who're you?
Prince:	I'm the messenger from beyond the sea.
King:	Have you brought any gift?
Prince:	I've brought what the rarest thing is in this land.
Knave:	Let's hear what it is.
Prince:	Trouble!
Six-pip Card:	Did you hear, did you hear him out? The man wants to advance! You won't believe me, the man laughs! In no time he'll lighten the whole atmosphere here.
Knave:	The atmosphere here is as still, as it is heavy; there's nothing quite like it in any planet. Even the Jupiter's thunder can't shake it, what else can you say?
All Cards:	(*Together*) What else can you say?
Knave:	If the flippant foreigner lightens the atmosphere here, then what'll happen?
King:	That's a matter to ponder.
All Cards:	That's a matter to ponder!
Knave:	Light weather is much prone to storm. If storm comes, the rules fly away. Then even our head-priest, Nine-pip Goswamy, will start saying: we will advance!
Five-pip Card:	Even, god forbid, laughter will perhaps become an epidemic here!
King:	O Knave of the Spades!
Knave:	Yes, Lord King?
King :	Aren't you the Editor?
Knave:	I 'm the Editor of the Lamp of Card Island. I'm the protector of Cultivation of the Card Island.
King:	Cultivation! What's it? It doesn't sound very sweet!
Knave:	No, my King, It is neither sweet nor very explicit; yet it's what's called novel, the newest attribute. This Cultivation is in danger today!
All Cards:	Cultivation, Cultivation, Cultivation!
King:	You must be having Editorial Columns?

Knave: Yes, two very long Columns!

King: Let the thunder from these two Columns stupefy everybody! We can't allow the climate of this land to become light!

Knave: We need a Compulsory Act!

King: What's that you said again?

Knave: It's the new lingo for the ear-pulling act. This too is among the newest contributions.

King: OK, this could be looked into later. Foreigner, is there any appeal from you?

Prince: Yes, there is, but not to you.

King: To whom?

Prince: To these Princesses!

King: OK, tell us.

Prince:

Song

O, serene, stony-figured, gracious one!
This restless self, from heart don't shun!
Come alone to the bower-wood,
Let tears in eyes mark the mood,
In crimson hues, let pain's bud
Have its colouring done!

Queen: What's this indiscipline, what's this injustice?

Five-pip Card: Give him banishment, Lord King, banishment

King: Banishment? Lady Queen, what's your opinion? Why are you silent? Could you hear me?

Queen: No, not banishment!

Ace Princesses: (*One by one*) No, not banishment!

King: Lady Queen, you seem to be a little distracted?

Queen: I myself feel distracted somehow!

Knave: Ace maidens, the beautiful Queen! Do remember, I've the Editorial Columns in my hands!

'Tasher Desh', Shadhona. Dhaka, Bangladesh

All Cards:	Cultivation, Cultivation, the Card Island's Cultivation! Save that Cultivation!
Knave:	Promulgate the Compulsory Act!
King:	That is?
Knave:	The ear-pulling act!
King:	I understand. Lady Queen, what's your view? Do I now promulgate the Compulsory Act?
Queen:	We also have our compulsory act in the inner precincts;—we shall see who gives whom banishment!
Ace Princesses:	*(All Together)* We'll promulgate the arbitrary illegal act!
Knave:	What's this happening? Alas Cultivation, alas Cultivation, alas Cultivation!
King:	I'm dissolving the Court. Let everybody move now. We can't safely stay here anymore! *(Exeunt the Band of Cards)*
Merchant:	My dear friend, I can't bear this place any longer! They're all aberrations of the divinity! If we stay among them, we'll be totally spoilt!
Prince:	Can't you see what's happening inside? Can't you see

the first stirring of life amidst the puppets? I'm not going to leave till I see to its end.

Merchant: But, it's like the cage of the living dead! They're all pickled in the digestive juice of rules!

Prince: Just open your eyes and look to the other side.

Merchant: Of course, the spell from beyond the seas seems to have been effective! Spreading her legs under the tree, the Nine-pip Spade-maiden is looking at the sky! The rules from here seem to have flown away!

Prince: She's listening to the footsteps of the Club-maiden from the sky. Our company at this point of time may not be quite to her liking. Let's go and move aside. *(Exeunt both)*

Scene Three

The Spade-maiden is busy in toiletry. Enters Ace.

Ace:

Song

Tell me, friend, tell me his name
In each of my ear,
Name that from vina's cascading notes we hear.
In spring's breeze in wood's way
That name'll dissolve in
Separated bird-duo's musical play
That name'll be mad in *Bakul's* perfume, sheer.

Or else, from friend's mouth to mouth, will run
That name: in a swinging stance, in great fun.
In full-moon-night when alone
To unreasonable disquiet, mind'll be prone,
That name I'll sing in melodies clear.

Spade-maiden: Dear, tell me what's this happening in the kingdom of Cards! What a breeze of madness those foreigners have brought! The mind's agitated all the time!

Ace: Yes, dear Spade-maiden, who'd have guessed barely two days back that the Cards would lose their racial identity and move around exactly like humans! Fie, fie, what a big shame!

Spade-maiden: Tell me, dear, this human-like behaviour: it's such a breach of customs! But this was started by that Heart-maiden. Haven't you noticed? Her demeanour these days are quite unstable, she absolutely apes the human style. She keeps forgetting how she should stand by whose side; the whole neighbourhood is reeking of shame. She has brought such disrepute to the land of Cards!

Enters Club-maiden.

Club-maiden: What's it, dear Ace-madam, I hear, you're spreading abuse about us all around! You're saying that we've lost our customs; we sit when rising is due, and rise when it is wont to sit!

Ace: So what's wrong if we‘ve told the truth? The wanton lady, now that your two cheeks are glowing, which colour is that? And, that stance of your eye-brows: from which foreign collyrium-creeper have you borrowed? This is not provided in the scriptures of the Card Kingdom over seven generations! Do you think that nobody would notice you at all?

Club-maiden: My, My, I'll die! That you have tagged with your friend, been sitting under the *Bakul* tree and running a whispering campaign into the ears all the time: is that what's catered for in the scripts of the Land of Cards? On the other side, the poor Knave, he can't get hold of his compatriot and is dying in repentance!

Spade-maiden: O dear madam, you won't have to lecture overmuch! The red tape that you've tied round your coiffeur is the one fit for strangling to death the rules and rituals of the land of Cards. What shameless-ness, despite being a Card-lady!

Club-maiden: So what of that! I'm not scared of anybody; the hide-and-seek like yours is not in my nature! Now that your Ten-pip Card-maiden came to pour scorn at me calling me a 'human female', I've given her a clear-cut answer: I would rather not die as a Card-woman than survive as human female.

Spade-maiden: Don't you have such vanity, please don't!—Do you know: there's already a word going round that you would be made into an outcaste.

Club-maiden: The caste of Cards I've discarded with my own hands, so what do I care!

Spade-maiden: How terrible! I haven't heard of a worse audacity in my seven generations! Here she is going to tom-tom that she is going to become a human! Let's go, Princes-Ace, people may see us from some sides and make out whom we're talking to, we'll be sunk then! *(Exeunt all)*

Scene Four

Enters the Heart Ace-maiden.

Heart-maiden:

Song

I came to pluck flowers in woods,

woods on the woods.

I don't know what happened to mood.
It was not plucking flowers,
it was not plucking flowers,
Get tearful, both eyes would.

Enters Diamond-king.

Diamond-king: What's it, Heart-maiden, you're here!

Heart-maiden: Why, what's happened, what do you want?

Diamond-king: Summons has come for you, to the Inner Circle of the palace.

Heart-maiden: Tell them that I've been lost.

Diamond-king: Lost?

Heart-maiden: Yes, I've been lost. You'll not get back again the one you're looking for, no longer.

Diamond-king: Goodness gracious, what an audacity! You've come to this forest! Don't you know—this is ruled out?

Heart-maiden: Yes, ruled out, but under which rules is this ensemble of clouds in the rainless land of cards? Suddenly I got up in the morning and saw that blue clouds have gathered across the sky. So long the peacocks of your land used to move with measured steps, why are they dancing with plumes all spread today?

Diamond-king: But, the one for whom even the courtyard outside home is foreign territory, has today come out to pluck flowers, how come such a bizarre activity has come to your mind?

Heart-maiden: I suddenly thought I was a gardener in the previous birth, used to plucking flowers. Today the eastern breeze bore the aroma of the flower-orchard from that birth. The honeybees from the *Madhavi*-garden from that birth have come humming in mind.

Song

The honey-bee came home with humming sound,
Whose news it wants me to hear going round?

In the light, in which sky,
In wood, myrtles wake up shy?
Message of blooms' awakening: it does redound!

How can at home place I find,
I'm so uneasy in mind—
How passes the day, so time-bound!

What illusions in their touch
All my jobs do besmirch!
Time passes as my tunes network found!
Whose news it wants me to hear going round?

Diamond-king: Well, I've been looking around for the Card-princesses for the Inner Circle, where are they—

Heart-maiden: Yes, they are all here, on the river-banks, under the trees.

Diamond-king: What are they up to?

Heart-maiden: They're changing dress, just like me. How do I look? Do you like it?

Diamond-king: It does seem that the curtains have been raised, clouds are removed from over the moon, they all are new beings altogether!

Heart-maiden: Your Six-pip, Five-pip Cards came over to admonish us, go over and see what their condition has been!

Diamond-king: Why, what happened?

Heart-maiden: They're moving around like crazy. They're sighing all the time; they're humming some songs even!

Diamond-king: Song? Six-pip and Five-pip Cards are singing songs?

Heart-maiden: If not in tune, out of tune at least! I was then making out my braid of hair. I couldn't stay too long, but leave the place.

Diamond-king: You surprise me! Making braid of hair! Who did you teach this skill?

Heart-maiden: No one. Just look there, rains have suddenly come in the dry fountains. The braiding of hair began with the cascading flow of waters. Who taught them this art? Come with me, let me sing you the song of Six-pip and Five-pip Cards. *(Exeunt both)*

Enter the Card-princesses.
Song and dance

Unknown tunes, who leaves in each of my ear?
Thoughts of mine float away in music clear.
In shadowy world of forgotten birth,
In remorse for the lost vina's dearth,
My melody keeps wailing having lost its way.
In which spring's union-night, to high stars dear
Thoughts of mine float away in music clear.

Enter again Diamond-king and Heart-maiden.

Diamond-king: Whom do I blame? Even I feel like singing!

Heart-maiden: Watch out, let the Editor not hear you, he'll put you in the Editorial Column. I found him prowling around to get the news of this forest. Look, Heart-maiden, my fear seems to have vanished, I don't know why. Order me to do something; I want to do something impossible for you.

Heart-maiden: Whatever else you do, don't sing a song please! Red china-roses have bloomed in the forest, fetch me some by plucking. I'll use their sap for colouring below the feet.

Diamond-king: Look, the beautiful one, ever since I got up this morning, I realised that our land of Cards is a dream;

it suddenly broke. Another birth of ours is floating around in the air. Its message is coming to the mouth, its melody is humming in the ear. Just listen, just listen, my own song created in that by-gone age is being ferried by somebody.

Song

Under your feet, let the colours loom,
In my mind's wood, in red notes' bloom.
So that in my songs' note-cascade
In your ear, I put jewel-grade,
So that gem-garland I string, loving soul to zoom.

Heart-maiden: This song you composed one day, and it was for my sake. How could you compose it?

Diamond-king: As you composed your hair's braid!

Heart-maiden: Well, can you recollect, I danced to your melody at some age?

Diamond-king: Yes, Yes, I can recollect. I really wonder how I had forgotten all this time!

Song

Frenzied winds have assailed my music's boat;
They give swing, they give swing
To your restive dance's waves that do float.
If the cord gets lopped,
If the radar is dropped,
Billowy waves are mopped
In front, if death looms too large,
I don't fear, I'll win, and I'll win by rote.

Diamond-king: Look, Heart-maiden, my mind has become restless in order to combat with the king of death. I can visualise the picture right in front of the mind's eye that you put in, on the of victory-mark on my forehead, I go out to rescue the damsel in distress, and sound my kettledrum before the closed gates of the fort. I can almost hear the song that you sang to bid me farewell.

Song

Bring victory-garland for my sake.
The long night, I'll remain awake.
When your steps fall on shore of death,
My soul will swing in heart's stealth,
If all's lost, I'll share your ruin's stake.

Heart-maiden: Come, come, my hero, let's both move together staking death. I can visualise as if there's a black stone's browbeat right in front, we've to demolish it. If it falls on the head, let it be. We'll have to carve our path by breaking through the heart of mountains. Why have we come here? It's a shame, we're wasting ourselves here. What meaningless days are here, what soulless nights! What a futile existence is swirling around every moment!

Diamond-king: Do you have courage, the beautiful one?

Heart-maiden: Yes, I have, I have!

Diamond-king: Won't you be scared of the unknown?

Heart-maiden: No, I won't be.

Diamond-king: The feet will be badly hurt, the way will be endless.

Heart-maiden: It was ages ago that we journeyed into that inaccessible terrain. I had held a lighted torch before you in the night, waived the victory-banner in front of you in the day. Stand up once again today, we'll have to break asunder the fencing of idleness, the boundaries of the lifeless; we'll have to push aside the debris of the worthless.

Diamond-king: Tear away the cover, tear it into bits and pieces. Be free, be pure, and be complete. *(Exeunt both)*

Enter Six-pip and Five-pip cards.

Six-pip Card: Dear Five-pip, tell me what's happening around?

Five-pip Card: I feel so ashamed to look at myself. Fool, fool! What were we doing so long?

Six-pip Card: After such a long time, the question's cropping up as to what all this means.

Five-pip Card: There comes the Ten-pip Scholar, let's ask him.

Enters the Ten-pip Card.

Six-pip Card: So long we were spending days: by rising and falling, lying and sitting, and by warbling around, what did it all mean?

Ten-pip Card: quiet!

Six-pip and Five-pip Cards (*Together*): We won't be quiet.

Ten-pip Card: Aren't you afraid?

Six-pip and Five-pip Cards (*Together*): We're not afraid, you have to tell us what all this means.

Ten-pip Card: There's no meaning,—It's the rule.

Six-pip Card: If we don't follow the rule?

Ten-pip Card: You'll be damned.

Six-pip Card: Let's be damned then!

Ten-pip Card: What'll you do, once damned?

Five-pip Card: If there's disrepute in the damnation, we'll fight against it.

Ten-pip Card: What kind of strong-headed talk is this in a peace-loving land!

Five-pip Card: We've resolved to violate peace.

Enters Heart-maiden.

Ten-pip Card: Did you hear this, Madam Heart-maiden? These worthies want to violate peace beside this fathomless Pacific Ocean?

Heart-maiden: Our state of peace is like the ancient tree. It is moth-eaten from inside, and has become lifeless; it needs to be cut down.

Ten-pip Card: Shame, shame, shame, shame, could you utter such a thing in your mouth? You're women, you should protect peace; we're men, we'd protect culture.

Heart-maiden: For much too long you have deceived us, Scholar-sir! It could no longer be done; your sap of peace has frozen our blood-stream. Don't you cheat us any more!

Ten-pip Card: How very terrible! From whom did you learn such language?

Heart-maiden: I'm calling him in my mind. I'm listening to his song throughout the sky!

Ten-pip Card: How awful! Song in the sky! This will vitiate the Land of Cards! One can't stay on here any longer. *(Exits)*

Six-pip Card: The beautiful one, it's you who should show us the way.

Five-pip Card: You have received the chant of discord, please teach us that chant!

Heart-maiden: We're alive in the curse of the gods, in the ignominy of foolishness. Come, let's move out.

Six-pip Card: For the slightest movement, they find fault, call us 'impure'.

Heart-maiden: Let there be fault, but there's nothing more impure than lying dead.

Exeunt all.

Spade-maiden and Ace-princess are plucking flowers.

Ace-princess: O my God, there comes the Ten-pip Lady. There can be no escape any more!

Enters the Ten-pip lady.

Ten-pip lady: Where are you hiding? O dear, you can't be recognised any longer! This seems to be our Ace. And, who is she, our Spade-maiden! My, my, I'll die in shame! What an appearance you've made of yourself! Have you become dressed as human dolls? Aren't you ashamed?

Ace-princess: I haven't dressed, the dress has got unhooked by sheer chance!

Ten-pip lady: The bonding of the Land of Cards is a rather tight one. There're thousands of knots tied over thousands of years, how could they just get unhooked! How did it happen?

Ace-princess: A gust of wind showed up.

Ten-pip lady: O dear, what're you saying? Could bonding get unhooked by a gust of wind? You are laying so much blame at the name of our god of winds! Another thing, is this a heretical land where a mere whiff of wind dislodges and flies away dry leaves of the tree?

Spade-maiden: Why don't you see with your own eyes, elder sister, what great changes have been wrought by our god of winds?

Ten-pip lady: Look, it ill behoves a small person to brag big! Our god of winds is so ancient! But then scriptures do mention that he has a very brave son, who apparently jumps around mighty high! Perhaps he has possessed you all!

Ace-princess: Why are you accusing only us? Haven't you noticed anything so far? He has been jumping across the whole land of Cards! He has set the hearts of Card-maidens afire!

Spade-maiden: The men from across the seas are claiming that it's he who is apparently their ancestor.

Ten-pip lady: It's just possible—they seem to be the progeny of a jumping clan.

Ace-princess: Well, could you please tell me the truth, elder sister—deep inside, hasn't your own mind got restless? No, you can't keep silent!

Ten-pip lady: Promise you won't tell anybody?

Ace-princess: Here I touch you and promise, I won't tell anyone.

Ten-pip lady: Last night in the early dawn I had a dream in my sleep: I've suddenly become human; moving around exactly like them. Once awake, I could die with shame! Yet --

Ace-princess: Yet what?

Ten-pip lady: Let it be.

Spade-maiden: We understand, quite understand; the caged bird of the day got her freedom in the dream!

Ten-pip lady: Quiet, quiet, quiet please, if the Ten-pip Scholar gets an inkling, he would make me atone even for the dream. Because, it was no doubt a sin. But, then what a very enjoyable dream!

Ace-princess: Whatever you may say, dear, the wind from across the seas is blowing real hard. We're unable to keep anything tied up any more, as it were; everything is flying away.

Ten-pip lady: Even then, some things have flown away, some still remain. If the veil overhead has dropped, the bent-anklets from the feet haven't become straightened as yet!

Spade-maiden: You've told the very truth; our mind is swinging across the seas from this side to the other. Just look there, the Club-maiden is so unbearably keen to become human, so she has put on a human mask—the one made at the workshop-room of the Card arena. How ludicrous it looks!

Ten-pip lady: We can't make out ourselves what we have begun to look like. I could overhear from behind the tree yesterday: the merchant's son was commenting that they're looking as grotesque imitations of humans.

Ace-princess: O dear, what a shame! What did the prince respond?

Ten-pip lady: He flared up and said that's all to the good—the taste has revealed itself from the dressing up. He said: don't laugh at that; if you want to laugh, then go and look at those among humans who move around by clowning like the Cards.

Spade-maiden: O dear, does that happen as well? Aping Cards despite being human! Well, what do they do?

Ten-pip lady: The prince was narrating that they dye their lips with painting sticks, use black lamp-soot to draw eye-brows, and much besides, quite akin to the dyed Cards. The funniest thing is that they wear hoofed leather under their feet.

Ace-princess: Why?

Ten-pip lady: It amounts to rising above, not touching earth with feet! These all are imitative of Cards, namely, painting and dressing up styles.

Spade-maiden: This looks like a topsy-turvy game of the god of wind! Cards seek to become human by discarding colours, while humans want to become Cards by putting on paint! I've, by the way, resolved to adopt the esoteric word to become human right from the Prince

Ace-princess: I, too.

Ten-pip lady: I, too, am keen, but apprehensive as well. I've heard that humans have much sorrow, but Cards have none of it.

Ace-princess: But I don't want to leave the fascination for that sorrow. From time to time the eyes overflow in tears, but why I can't fathom.

Song

Why eyes overflow in tears,
Why have I unease in mind –

As if some sudden words I find,
I forget them, in mind still I find.
As if at one's promise
Pain did increase,
As if has gone away, someone unkind—
This neglect left soul hurt behind.
As if some sudden words I do find,
I forget them, in mind still I find.

Spade-maiden: Get lost, everybody get lost, there comes the Editor. If it's publicised in the press, we can in no way show face.

Ten-pip lady: Right there the whole gang is coming. The Court will be held under the old margosa tree. We can't stay here any longer, *(Exeunt all)*

Enter King, Courtiers, etc.

King: This place seems a little odd. What's that smell there?

Five-pip Card: Of *Kadamba* flower.

King: *Kadamba,* an extraordinary name! What's that bird calling?

Five-pip card: I've heard that it's called dove.

King: Dove! Give it a proper name; you can call it 'Civility'.—It has become difficult to carry on with any activities. Today the sky is reverberating with words; the wind is resonant with melody. With great effort I've kept the mind composed. I found it difficult to keep the Queen confined at home; she's dancing around, as if possessed by ghosts! Dear members, it's difficult to recognise you today—you are not attired properly for the court, but dressed most uncivilly.

All cards: It's nobody's fault. Our attires have become loose;

they've slipped down on their own—they all are lying across the streets.

King: Editor, even you seem to lacking in solemnity.

Knave: Since morning I've been roaming in the woods, collecting names of the truant females; I've been infected by its breeze. While filling up the Editorial Column, I noticed that rhythm was oozing out of my writing pen. I've heard that it's such effusion that's called 'influenza'.

King: What kind is it?: let's have an instance.

Knave:

In the land where orders violate
The mandatory rules forsooth,
In that land, Ten-pip keeper of truth
How can safeguard culture's border?—
That land's destined for disorder!

King: Stop, there's no need for anymore. Introduce it in the fourth-graders' text-book. Let the children of the Card Community learn it by rote.

Six-pip Card: Lord King, we're not students of infant section of your Fourth Grade. Today we suddenly realised that we've come of age. This rhythm does not hold water.

King: O dear foreigner, could you put into our ears rhythms of the overseas?

Prince: Yes, I could. Listen then.

Song

Across skies goes clarion call:
Lightning-loading, thunder-foreboding:
Vaishakhi in thrall!
Rhythms of a daring tempo
Pulsate in big fig tree;
Frenzied by void's ambrosia, ever so free:

Catching rhythm of unknown ways
In moving wings, birds enthrall!

Heart's inside they churn and bide
In the black-and-white divide,
In the good and the snide,
In straight and in oblique stall.
Rhythms dance in oblation's fiery wave,
In heartbeats of freedom-fighters: brave,
Rhythms rush in apocalypse's
Fierce chariot's footfall.

King: Could you understand anything?

All Cards: No, nothing.

King: Then?

All Cards: Mind went mad!

King: That's no good. Just listen to an incantation from our ancient scripture—

The one who is calm:
God of death turns him around
After handling, throws him as found,
Saying: "To me, you're unwelcome".
Listen, dear foreigner!

Prince: Do command.

King: You're roaming around restlessly all over the Card island—plunging into the waters, climbing to the top of the hills, using axe to carve pathways into the forests—why are you doing all this?

Prince: Lord King, you all are always getting up and sitting down, turning on sides and turning back, why are all that as well?

King: That's according to rules.

Prince: This is according to our wishes!

King: Wish? How terrible! Wish in this land of Cards! Friends, what do you say to that?

Six-pip and Five-pip Cards: We've adopted the chant of wish from them.

King: Which chant?

Six-pip and Five-pip Cards:

Song

Desire:

It does breaking, it does making,
It accepts or throws far.
It's the one which strikes at lock,
Tearing bondage to flee the flock,
Again it returns to the confine of bar!

King: Go, go, go away from here, go away soon. Heart-maiden, didn't the words reach the ears? Spade-maiden, did you notice her behaviour? Why is all this happening so suddenly?

Heart-maiden: Wish!

Other Aces: Wish!

King: What's that, Lady Queen, you got up so fast?

Queen: I can't keep sitting any more!

King: I doubt, Lady Queen, your mind has become restless.

Queen: There's no doubt that it's restless.

King: Do you know, restlessness is the worst crime in the land of cards?

Queen: I know, and I know too that it's the most pleasurable thing.

King: What's a punishable thing, you're calling a pleasurable thing! Have you forgotten the very language of the land of Cards?

Queen: In the language of our land of Cards, Chains are called ornaments, it's now time of forget such language!

Diamond: Yes, Lady Queen, in this language the prison is called the father-in-law's house!

King: Shut up!

Heart-maiden: They call quizzes the scriptures!

King: Shut up!

Heart-maiden: The dumb is called the saint!

King: Shut up!

Heart-maiden: The fool is called the scholar!

King: Shut up!

Five-pip Card: They call the dead the living!

Queen: And, the heaven is called the haven of guilt! Please shout everybody: victory to the wish!

All Cards: Victory to the wish!

King: Lady Queen, you're exiled to forests.

Queen: I'm saved then.

King: Banishment!—What's that, where are you going?

Queen: To banishment.

King: Will you leave me behind?

Queen: Why should I leave you behind?

King: Then?

Queen: I'll take you alongside.

King: Where to?

Queen: To banishment.

King: And all these, my subjects?

All Cards: We'll go to banishment!

King: Ten-pip Scholar, what do you think?

Ten-pip Scholar: I think the banishment smacks good.

King: And how about your scriptures?

Ten-pip Scholar: I'll float them away in the waters.

King: The Compulsory Act?

Ten-pip Scholar: It won't hold any more.

All Cards: It won't hold, it won't hold!

Queen: Where are those humans gone?

Prince: Here we are.

Queen: Can we become humans?

Prince: Of course, you can.

King: O dear foreigner, can I become too?

Prince: I doubt. But the Queen is there as your aid. Victory to the Queen!

Choral song

Break, bonds break down, bonds break down,
bonds break down, break,
Captured heart-soul let wings take.

In dry Ganga let run
Life's flood in wayward fun—
Victory-songs of breakage, make.

Let old and worn-out float away,
Do float away, do float away.

We've heard it clear: Don't fear, don't fear, don't fear,
It's call for new to stay.
Unknown doesn't us, upset,
At its closed down gate, rush fast at your stake.

* * *

Shapmochan

(Deliverance From Curse)

Foreword

There's a song for the foreword. The idea is this; the mind's many deep desires compose figures in the story in the form of rhythmic bonds, give company to imagination, and—getting dissociated momentarily from the material world—play into the world of the imagery.

It's only an idle foray—it's mere cloud's play,
It's sheer mental wish consigned to wind;
It's absent-minded weaving garland to tear away,
Momentary laugh and cry: into music to rescind.
Atop on green leaves in summer the whole time
With their own shadows, playful are the flowers;
It's also that shadow-play in the spring's breeze,
As if willfully losing way in mystery's bowers
Roaming whole day here'n'there unhurriedly at ease
As if to gift someone, blooms're picked from some towers,
Forest's flowers in evening fly back to forest's lease.
Who'd play this game, alas, who's playmate nearby,
Forgetfully I sing songs—some listen some don't listen—
If something is remembered, if someone comes well nigh.

The celestial performer Sourasen was among the vanguard in the divine court. The other day his beloved Madhushri had gone to the North Pole to go round the sun. Sourasen's mind—separated from her—was a little distracted. Lacking attention, his drum's rhythm missed a beat; the dancing Urvashi's time-cycle stopped short of the rhythmic end; the divine queen's forehead went red.

Lest I forget the tune, this is the fear,
Lest the broken string gets victory dear.
Lest the festive hour
In lazy sleep does cower,
The sacred moment sheer
Disdainful play does tear;
Lest the union-time sans song does bear.

When in frenzied dance I'm called in,
Lest my steps in that storm's rhythm
Don't at all sync;
When death will send at the end its welcome-song,
Lest in life, long
My words all disappear,
Lest sans song, farewell-moment does disappear.

The divine court, having missed its rhythm, cursed the celestial performer's body to be disfigured; he was to be born as Aruneshvar at the royal home of the Gandharas.

Madhushri came and laid her head at the foot-rest of the divine queen to appeal: "Please don't make us separated, Goddess, let's have our destination in the same land,—in suffering from the same sorrow, in the same ignominy".

The divine queen looked with sad eyes at the divine king. Said the latter," OK, go to earth, you'll get misery there, and cause misery. That suffering will mitigate the guilt of the missing rhythm".

Farewell song

Let farewell's cup put memory's nectar in harness,
In union's festive fair, do return it with due grace.
In tears to bid good-bye,
In inmost heart, let it lie,
And covertly fructify heart's own message fresh.

The way you've to go, you're quite lonely there –
In eyes dark does flow, in prayers light shines fair.
In whole day's solitary gap,
Put in mind nectar's sap,
At lotus-wood in soul's lap, separation's deity has access.

*

Madhushri was born in the royal family of the Madra's, with the name of Kamalika. The pangs of separation that Aruneshvar was carrying with him from the heavens became acute in his youth.

In wakefulness passes night—
From eyes of mine, sleep took flight.
For whom I move all alone—
Eyes're thirsty, he has not shown,
His flute, oh dear, it's his flute, his flute fills my heart's full might.

There's no word, yet whispering
What I hear: none knows a thing.
In this heart full of pain, In eye-lids: moist with rain,
Shadow swings, its shadow swings, shadow swings at day-night's plight.

The scorched heart was in quest of water to quench thirst in the prevailing drought, and sang with vina on the lap:

O water of thirst, come gushing in,
Pierce the solid's chest's jutting chin:
With murmurs, warbling din.
Come, come from the source
From deep dark, close
Come you, O clean:
With murmurs' warbling din.

Sunrays keep waiting for you,
You're the playmate: it longs for your view.
Its golden tunes' cascade
In you, melody shed,
Come, O bright gleam:
With murmurs' warbling din.

Relentless winds do shout:
Come, come, come, it seeks you out.
For its drums' deep sound,
To clap, you're bound,
Come, O mobile lean:
With murmurs' warbling din.

Drought with its illusive power
Has imprisoned you in stony tower.
Breaking the sapless jail
Come in chainless trail,
Come, O mighty clean:
With murmurs' warbling din.

Kamalika's portrait somehow reached the royal interiors of the Gandharas. It seemed, what went lost in this birth, had as if come back to be caught in an ethereal dream.

O my dear moonshine, in evening of *Fagun* today
You've let self be trapped in your leaves, branches gay.
Music in your tune's flow
Floods stars as they glow,
In my yard rings that tune: in my soul's rhythms' sway.

All my buds bloom forth at the hint of your smile,
Dream in freeze, in south breeze, runs amuck in blooms' scent's guile.

O white, you do dishevel,
Hues' swing in my soul's sail,
My murmuring heart's entwined in web-of your laughter's way.

The portrait held its sway on his thoughts of the day and dreams of the night.

Are you a picture mere, drawn on sheer canvas?
That vast distant nebular mass
Which does congest the sky's nest,
And those who're, day and night,
Wayfarers to dark with beacons of light planets, stars, sun, and the rest,
Aren't you as true as they're?
Alas, picture, you're mere portrait.

You don't face the eye,
Within the eye now you lie—today thereby
You're green with the green, blue with the blue.
My earth in you
Has found its inmost clue.
I don't know, nobody does know –
In my song, your melody does blow.
In the poet's heart, you're the poet –
Not portrait, not portrait, no sheer portrait.

The king sent a missive to the embodiment of the portrait. He wrote—

When did you put in the dream garland of gloom,
With welcome-bloom?
I woke to find in morn
In red cloud drawn
Farewell-flute in wails does loom.
You came in secret, I didn't see with eyes set,

With sorrow's cord in dark,
You bound me stark,
Adorned me with garbs singed in sorrow of loom.

The letter reached the princess. Her mind became restive at the beckoning of the unknown. She read the letter over and again with her companions.

Do read me out, you all, what he's written to me,
Let the touchstone of his scripted message in my soul, pervaded be.
Let the aroma of field of corn
In lonely home be borne,
Tired slow wayfaring breeze may touch my open hair with glee.

Borrowing the tune of blue sky, let it strum in my lonely mind,
Stoic colour of the dusty road, let my window do find.
In the sun-set's reddened hours,
I'll spread soul in game's colours,
In own mind, in corner of eyes, tears' hints will be there to see.

Gandhara's messenger reached the capital of the Madra's. Listening to the wedlock proposal, the king said, "It's my daughter's rare luck". Companions went to the princess to say—

Play, my friend, the flute will play.
In heart, heart's lord will adorn gay.
Torrents of words
Will flow outwards,
Shy smile on lips will flicker to stay.
In moist eye, tear
Will then appear,
Pain of delight, in mind shall lay.
Fainting in mind,

Heart'll seek to bind,
Touching pair of feet to pray.

In the *Chaitra* full-moon's sacred moment was the auspicious time. On that nuptial night, the king—sitting far by himself—had blood surge in his heart. He kept recalling how, in a different land, he swung with someone in a similar moon-lit night. From out of the mist of forgetfulness, a stanza was humming in his mind: 'Don't forget,—don't forget,—don't forget'—

We both that day swung in wood-bay, tying flower-garland in swing,
Memory of that kind keeps alive in mind, every moment, not forgetting.

That day in wind was fulsome,
You know, with my delirium,
From sky to sky, echoes had come: of your laughter's ring.

Going on the way in night gay—full moon was in the sky,
Your and mine was a meet fine: a pious moment, well-nigh.
Now time's gone, I'd alone have separation's burden borne—
Tie on your hand that I did adorn: don't please let it sling.

At the right time—seated on the jewelled back of a royal elephant—arrived the vina from king Aruneshvar's own lap: as the royal representative, carrying the unheard summon of the king. Companions sang the welcome-melody for the far-away king—

Your delight: at the doors, please, do please throw,
O my townsmen.
From bosom your clothes-end,
On dusty yard please throw.
On road scented water do spray,
Lest his feet are soiled by clay,

Your beautiful one, at the gates, deigns to go—
Fervent heart in front of him, dear: strew to grow.

All are blessed, are blessed to know:
For universe's welfare today, open doors do show.
Witness: crimson is all the sky,
Heart goes happy on the sly,
Your constant light on the doors do please throw –
Your soul's lamp do lift up: in that light, let show.

Welcoming the vina, denizens of the inner palace brought it to the marriage platform and sang as their call to the bride—

O dear flute, do please play.
Beauteous one, in sandal-garland on sacred evening, adorn gay.
Perhaps in month of *Falgun* sweet,
Restless wayfarer does greet,

Shapmochan, Pallavi, Dhaka, Bangladesh. Photo: Pankaj Kumar.
pg 65: Shapmochan, Pallavi, Dhaka, Bangladesh. Photo: Pankaj Kumar.

Has Champak, quivering under bees feet,
On the yard, bloomed today?

On head red garbs do stand,
Guelder-rose bangles're on hand,
Anklets' rhyme on the feet,
In aroma winds retreat,
Welcome-song, resonating along,
On Eden-grove, heralds stay.

Garlands were exchanged between the princess and the vina. Dedicating the vina to the beautiful, the companions sang—

Please pick up, do pick up silent vina serene,
From garden of heaven, let its tunes glean,
O beautiful, my beautiful.
I've spread darkness in the night-sky,
Hoping you'd come by.
In stars have your lit-up message: let its glow be seen,
O beautiful, my beautiful.

My stone-block in deep woe wails to you and say—
Let your caress give good grace, with tears sweeping away,
O beautiful, my beautiful.
This arid desert naked, daily dies in shame,
In my heart lame.
Its clothes-end in green sap: pull over its bosom clean.

When the bride was leaving for the groom's home, companions paid obeisance to the beautiful and said—

Do redden in your dye, ere you go.
In your dye, on the sly,

In bright smile, in slight wile,
In flow of tears that sadly rile.
Let your colours touch my heart—
Let it besmirch my chores' chart—
Let it burn in evening lamp –
Put on wakeful night its stamp.

Before you part, make me alert,
Sway your feet to rock my heart.
As stars're wakeful in dark night,
In stone-cave's pool is spring's sprite;
As in cloud's bosom, cloud's chant's awake,
At core of world's dance, rhythm's at stake—
So you do swing me on,
On departure's way anon,
Wailing, quelling all begone!

*

The royal bride came to the consort's abode.

No lamps were lit, the chamber remained dark; in that chamber every night the bride came to be united with the husband.

Kamalika urged, "Lord, my day, my night are eager to see you. Do please appear before me".

Do come to my home;
Do come out: the one, who within heart do roam.
Do open dream-doors to come out in morn's sunlight,
In these eyes' delight.
From the hint of transience in eternity's dome, Do come to my home.
Come in joy and sorrow's swings.
Come bearing on life's waves' wings.
You were in hope's formless message in *Fagun*'s breeze
Which wood's eager breath did seize—

Now in flowers' pleasant form, come on heart's tome.

The king said, "Do see me in my songs. First see me in your inmost heart; the day to see me outside will come afterwards. Otherwise there'll be an error, the rhythm will be broken".

Where too far out on winged clout, alas, it flies away.
Your roving eyes do surprise, escaping into wood gay.
Oh dear, in your heart when tunes start to flow flute's sweet muse,
Then on its own, it'll bemoan and welcome the hanging noose—
Then it won't fritter in nervy glitter in wanton moves, to stay.

You don't even look in heart's nook who wanders to and fro—
You in ears, hear message clear borne by south-breeze flow.
Today scents from bloom dispels gloom in happy, fervent song,
As if eternal spring has come looking for you, surging along,
Perhaps your quest outside in haste seems like a madcap play—
Alas, those eyes, like birds, fly escaping into woods gay.

The vina played in the dark. The groom went round the bride in the dark with the dance-form of celestial arts. That art-form had come down to his mortal body as companion of the exile. The dance's sorrow hit the queen's bosom, like the high tide rising in the sea in the midnight, inundating with tears.

One night at the evening's third-quarter hour, the lode-star was in the eastern sky; Kamalika covered the both the king's feet with her unbraided hair; she said, "Command me to witness you in the first light of the dawn. Otherwise, let me bid farewell, leaving my wail in the heart of this darkness—as long as you don't beckon me back into your lit-up court".

I've come to doors of her room,
Called her in the gloom,
Holding the bolt I shook to try,

Hours went, without reply,
I didn't get to see her loom.

But before I recede from here
I'd leave this message clear.
Whether I see you or not,
Know this: I came to this spot,
To distant shore, I'd zoom.

Said the king, "Beloved, don't spoil the deep mystique of the un-seeing, this is my appeal. You're still in two minds, time for the sacred meeting of eyes haven't arrived yet".

O the absent-minded one,
Carrying the garland of my words to you, won't be done.
It'll be futile: message mine,
My truth, when will you divine?
I won't know your mind's run.
If the moment favours evening's silent sweet peace,
When your eyes're dripped in cheerless light's bliss.
I'll offer you solace in serene tune's turn.

In your ears, rhymed words I'll commune In slow tender tune;
As cricket in Sal-wood's sleepy night stark
Hums its ceaseless tune in chant's garland of dark—
In soul's lonely yard, I, alone,
Sitting in rapt attention
Will draw ritual design in musical fun.

The queen said, "Will both my eyes remain deprived forever from their favourite offering? It seems to be a curse even worse than blindness!"

Responded the king, "You could imagine any which way. That imagination will be the truth".

In wounded vanity, the queen turned her face.

Said the king, "Tomorrow is the last day of Chaitra. It's the day of my dance with companions in the privacy of the *Nagakeshar* wood. Look out from the palace-top".

The queen heaved a sigh. She asked, "How shall I recognise?"

The king said, "Do imagine any which way. Your imagination itself will be the truth".

Alas, dear, can you know him at all?
Eyes keep on seeking him, no address it can call.
In unseen paths to and fro,
I hear foot-falls come and go,
Only the breeze carries aroma: as the mark to stall.

How can I let him know,
I'm seated at road-side show?
In the soul evening came, In light and shadow's coloured game,
Spreading its bedstead where *Bakul* flowers fall.

*

Today open is the south gate,
Come my spring come, do come.
Heart's swings oscillate,
Come my spring, do come.
Come in comely green chariot,
Come on *Bakul* flower-laden spot,
Come playing ardent reed,
Come with Piyal blooms' scented seed,
Come my spring come, do come.

Come in dense leaves' shower, come dear.
Come in wild jasmine-bower, come dear.
In soft-sweet-wily smile
Come in wild breeze's land awhile—

Your own restless stole
You let fly in winds whole,
Come my spring, do come.

In the night of *Chaitra's* last day was there union again. The queen commented, "I saw the dance. It was like the impatience of the spring breeze in the *Sal* tree-rows. It was as if there was a storm in the fortnight before the full moon. But why was there an ugly one who brought disharmony? He seemed to be the disciple of the truncated demon! What was his qualification to gain entry there?"

The king kept silent. Then he sang away, "The beauty beckons in the prime pain of the unpleasant. The sunrays set the rainbow

Shapmochan, Pallavi, Dhaka, Bangladesh. Photo: Pankaj Kumar.

on the forehead of the dark cloud, for consoling its shame. When heaven's compassion descends to meet earth's curse, there appears the graceful. My beloved, didn't that very compassion sweeten your heart yesterday?"

"No, I can't tolerate distortion of the sap", responded the queen, getting up from her throne.

The king held her hand to say, "One day you'll be able to bear him out of your own heart's bounty. In the sacrifice of the ugly is the fulfillment of the beautiful".

Knitting her brows said the queen, "I can't fathom your sympathy for the unpleasant. Just listen to the coos of the morning's first cuckoo. It's her own feeling for light within darkness. At the sunrise-moment of this morning, let your manifestation be within my day: I'll wait in that hope".

The king sang—

When outer error'll disappear,
Will mind's mistake go?
Having burnt on grief's passion,
Sap's offering: will it know?
After sun-burn is over,
Will downpours come to hover?
After shame's tinge end in heart,
Will love's colour on it show?

The more you move far away,
The more the bonding becomes strong: won't the pain have its sway?
On dark clouds of self-esteem,
Rainy winds will hit full steam,
Won't torrential flow of tears allow any obstacles to grow?

The queen kept silent. The king said, "Well, I'll keep your promise; but that won't fulfill your desire".

The lights came on, the covers disappeared and the meeting took place. It shook the duo's life. Exclaiming, "What a huge deception!" the queen ran away from the chamber. The king called him from his world—

Don't go please, don't go at all.
We're athirst for union, keep words to call.
Till today, *Bakul's* oblivious of its own, oh alas,
Blooming of flowers is not yet done, basket isn't full,
O wayfarer, steps do stall.

*

He went away quite far, moving to the isolated palace that was meant for the hunting in the forest. He was overwhelmed by shame, like the lodestar covered by mist.

When the night had advanced to the second quarter, she heard, half-asleep, the lamentation-melody from a vina's tune. In dream reached the gestures from quite far. It appeared that the melody was an ever-familiar one. The tears of the eternally-separated one surged inside bosom.

O my friend, in darkness alone, I'm not consoled in mind,
In which thirst where'll he depart? The way he can't find.
In flowing stream, in dark too dim, in moist wind's gleam, dear,
To bring whose words into soul: to bind, at times unbind!

Night passed after night. The human who danced in the shadow of the tree could not be seen, but his heart could be perceived— in the swinging branches of the lonely deodar forest, carrying as though the loud wailing of the sea-breeze. The queen thought in mind: when he came near, it was a dark night. When the moon was up, his garland remained, but he was not there.

When you came in the dark,
Across sea-shore, moon didn't lark.
O unknown, I did then
Through perception, had your ken,
On soul's strings your caress from song did embark.

When alone you went away,
In night's lap the moon lay.
Then near road I did look
To see your garland lying in nook—
By guess, I realised to whom this necklace you did mark.

What happened to the royal queen? Which pang of parting was keeping her separation awake? Which bird—vigilant at night—flew past fast alongside, with its wings' swish making the sleeping bird's wings flutter?

The vina played the *ragas Kedara, Behag,* as also *Kalangda*. In the skies were the stars, like the silent chants of dark female ascetics. The vina-tunes no longer seemed playing outside, but pervaded her inmost heart's every little fibre.

Behold, there the flute does play
In wood's or in mood's way?
Wind of spring: where's it blowing where've flowers had bloomed?
Tell, friend, in sight: this happy night has risen in which bay?
In wood's or in mood's way?

Shall I go or not go:
The thought's too low;
I die in vain, in fear-shame to say,
Where, I won't know,
On tryst did he go:
in separation's utter disarray?
In wood's or in mood's way?

Shapmochan, Pallavi, Dhaka, Bangladesh. Photo: Pankaj Kumar.

The royal queen sat up on her bed: with her braid dishevelled, her bosom shivering. The vina's murmuring threw a limitless way of trysting, open in the sky. Her mind moved along that way in the void, laden with melody.

But it was towards whom? It was him whom she had known before the encounter, but had forgotten after the encounter.

One day the perfume of margosa flowers carried an invitation from the indescribable into the dark chamber. The queen left the bed to stand before the windows. Below was the dance on: of that shadowy figure, along with the swinging waves of separation.

Did he appear, didn't he appear? It wasn't clear.
Was he illusion, a dream-like vision, was he a deception, sheer?
Does he get caught in grace's knot?
Will music's notes put him in a spot?
He's in eternal separation's sphere.

In his flute is a plaintive tune,
In separation-union's melody it does commune.
In weal and woe, in getting, not getting,
He's a stoic wind in mind's wood-setting,
Perhaps he's an utmost desire, mere!

The queen's whole body was trembling. The night was filled with murmurs of cricket. The moon, in the fortnight before the new moon, was waning in the horizon. In dim light, the woods seemed to be whispering in dreams. The mute forest's wordless language touched all limbs of the queen. She didn't know when she began dancing. The dance seemed to belong to some other world, some other birth.

On the vina played the glides of the *raga Paraj*. Kamalika said in her own mind, "O the distressed, O the depressed one, don't call any longer. There'd be no more delay, no more delay".

Shapmochan, Pallavi, Dhaka, Bangladesh. Photo: Pankaj Kumar.

The moon of the fortnight before the new moon had disappeared. The call of the dark was intense. The royal queen rose up to say, "Ill go today. I'm no longer scared of my vision".

Trampling on the dry leaves by feet, she reached the banyan tree —under which the vina was playing.

My vina in which tune does play,
In which new agile rhyme?
My heart is trembling today,
In universal heart's own prime.
There comes which restless youth—
Flying his yellow garb in booth?
In light's dancing forsooth
Woods have a rollicking time!

In sky's vast expanse,
In soundless anklet's humming:
In the unheard rhythm's nuance,
Clapping leave-clusters're strumming!
Hopes of whose feet's caress
Have given grass sonorous phrase?
Bondless winds are listless
In which wood's aroma sublime?

The vina stopped.
The queen suddenly paused.
The king said, "Don't get scared, beloved, don't get scared".
His voice was like the distant thunder of the water-laden cloud.
"I'm no longer scared, victory is yours," said the queen and brought out the lamp from under her clothes-end. Slowly, she lifted it before the king's face.
Her voice choked, her eyes were listless.
She spoke up," My lord, my beloved, how beautiful you are!"

How wonder-struck I am, looking at you,
Where have you arrived from: to land in heart due?
That face and that laugh: Why do I love enough?
Why do I quietly surf in tearful view?
Why witnessing you, memory is rife:
You're all enduring, eternal in life.
If you don't stand coming en route,
In heart, doesn't play flute—
All lights, laughs absolute drown in dark's core.

* * *

Chitrangada

(The Manipuri Princess)

Foreword

Morning's indistinct primal presence is in a red-hued cover of glow.
Half-asleep eyes get their first inspiration ever.
At the end, piercing its crimson envelope, it comes brightly out in the awakened world In own stainless white.

Thus the initial state of truth comprises its exterior adornments,
In a variety of colours –
Its attraction overwhelms the uncultured mind.
Once the external cover opens up, its full manifestation occurs in the enlightened mind.

This is the essence of reality of the play Chitrangada.
Its dramatic narrative has –
The nascent lover's bonding with illusive ardour,
And then its relief from that delusion
Into the unadorned glory of the inherent truth.

Pleased at the devotion of the king of Manipur, Lord Shiva had bestowed the boon that only male children would be born in the family. Nevertheless, when Chitrangada was born in the royal clan, the king gave her the upbringing as a son. The princess practised archery. She learnt war strategy, principles of royal governance.

Arjuna (one among Panch-Pandavas) had adopted a vow of remaining an ascetic for twelve years and had come to Manipur during his sojourn.
This play begins then with a song.

The infatuating illusion has come,
Come in the youth's woody arbour.
It has come to haunt the heart,
Come in secret steps apart,
Come in golden-hued veneer in the dark, to start.

It has laid its magical noose,
In wind's blow, in shady show,
Playing the flute's muse.
It tests courage of the brave,
The sage's meditation it does stave,
The net of disaster
Encircled it from all sides, alert.

Come unadorned beautiful best,
Come the truth modest –
Attack dream's fort,
Bring, bring freedom, have its import –
Shredding deception's bondage,
Come to retrieve virility, smart.

Scene One

In this scene, there is preparation for Chitrangada going for a hunt, with a song.

Rumbling, rumbling, rumbling. rumbling,
deep clouds thunder on mountain-peaks,
Woods are shaded dark.
In the noise of fountain's gurgling sound,
Hunter's footsteps can't be heard by the scared
Deer-duo.
The chequered tiger has left its pug-marks on muddy path,
Leaving the trace of each footstep to its hiding cave.

Arjuna is asleep on the village-track.
Mistaking him as tiger to be hunted,
the companions chase him.

Arjuna:

Oh, what an intolerable impudence!
To Arjuna, whoever shows irreverence,
Where can he get his shelter?

Chitrangada: Arjuna! You're Arjuna!

Observing the companions clad as boys, Arjuna decides to ignore them.

Arjuna:

Ho-ho-ho-ho, ho-ho-ho-ho-ho, you brand of urchins,
Go for sap to mother's lap—don't you get scared.
Oh dear, what great fun!

Exits Arjuna.

Chitrangada, Darpana, Ahmedabad, India.

pg 87: Chitrangada, Nandonik Dance Academy, New Jersey, USA.

Chitrangada:

Arjuna! You're Arjuna!
Come back, come back—
Don't show contempt by showering pardon,
In direct combat, do me beckon!
The pride of hero's hand, to make me die
I want to vie—
Arjuna, You're Arjuna!

*

Alas, the wretched one, what a welcome from the great!
The god of your world did come,
And depart,
Leaving you, deceiving your heart—
Arjuna! You're Arjuna!

Companions:

Time passes away, do please say:
Which forest we'll go for-hunting?
Under dark cloud, in winds moist,
The deer flock to bamboo-wood shade to get rest.

Chitrangada:

Leave it, leave it, why's this false game?
On life comes aversion,
On myself is the shame.

Her self-inspirational song

Oh, let the storm come,
On my dry-leaves' branches,

Let the storm come,
At the rains arriving in new greens awesome!
Go the callous, go soulless, go the joyless one,
In final night's tears' torrents, let all be undone—

Whatever to go let go, in dance-rhythm not calm!

We've to spread our seats in empty soul's room,
And to wear new garbs on tearful heart's gloom.
Stream's waters have been flooded, overflowing bay—
Jasmine-wood's perfumed message has run far away—
My soul is awake perhaps behind death gruesome.

Companions:

Friend, what's the sight that you've seen?
In a momentary strike,
Has your old identity blown away?
At the glance of the sunray, has the bud's cover disappeared
And *Madhavi* recognised self very first time? .

Chitrangada:

My love, my eyes are touched by which light?

(Song)

Perhaps you were in sunray's expression bright!
My mind was perhaps awaiting you:
Through ages, in nights and days, all due,
Waiting in heart's deep anguished dark—
Many births passed in parting's plight.

Unbloomed spirits in grove and wood,
Sans tunes, were in saddened mood
Without friends, night's eternal pain
Can I pass in lone bed, lain?
O beautiful, the beauteous one,
Welcome-garland: have it spun, you have it spun.
Removing veil's unwholesome shade
See, shy smiling face in pure sight.

Exeunt all.

Enters Arjuna with forest companions and dances.

Scene Two

Companions sing.

Go, go, if you've to go then—
Yet you've to return again—
Again, again.
In tears' flow in vain
I won't be lain, won't be lain on dusty floor.
Putting off lamps I won't go outdoor,
For life's bright bargain.

My meditation is not in fear,
My strength'll be free, if doors're not clear.
Of averted moment, I've no scare—
Victory'll be done, I declare,
Over the days your heart's tied cords
I'll untie in love's glory plain.

Enters Chitrangada with companions for bath and sing.

Chitrangada:

All the while, in mind's pile I hear
Fathomless waters' call.
Mind doesn't stay, doesn't stay, doesn't stay at home,
Doesn't stay—Life does enthrall.

I'll float astride In high tide,
In flows submerging all thoughts, I'll bathes till.

Chitrangada, Darpana, Ahmedabad, India.

Burn of vain desires will then pall.

Waves in waters grow—
Waves flow, waves flow, in heart's core waves do flow.
What's this impatience in the sky, in winds sly?
As if ardent fairy's scarf in romance does sprawl.
On seashore far,
Whose anklets stir to have a ball?

She sings addressing the companions.

Come you all, re-new myself, in ornaments new.
In the frost's curse was bereft the distressed forest-land—
In spring, let depression go, new charm to imbue;
Let empty branches forget shame with leaves' cover a-new.

Companions:

Let love's illusive chant absolute
Play on happy soul's instrument lute
Greeting the eternally beautiful.
Let delighted ripples of dance

On limbs, keep spreading trance:
In wave after wave,
With the desired, let youth gather respect with union due.

Exeunt all.

Arjuna enters and sits in meditation. Encircling him, Chitrangada sings and dances.

Chitrangada:

I will surrender to you
With heart-soul-mind due.

Arjuna:

Do forgive me—forgive me—
I'm not fit to be adored, O excellent maiden—with my vowed abstinence.

Exits Arjuna.

Chitrangada:

Alas, alas, I've failed my femininity
In this prolonged life of mine.
Shame to the bow and arrow!
Shame to the might of arms!
A moment's forceful flood of tears
Has floated out my worship of manhood.
The sigh of unfulfilled youth
Has made spring all impatience!

Chitrangada sings with companions.

Such a weeping spring, friend, perhaps ne'er entry did make,
Guilder rose's crimson colours, parting's pangs did take.

Companions:

Your *Baishakh* had sun's scorching burn,
When rains carry over *Asadh* in turn!
Alas, Alas, Alas!

Chitrangada:

In arbour-gate, the wild jasmine
Has got adorned with new leaves green,
All day and night, in listless sheen,
Looking for whom, it remains awake?

Companions:

Within hard stones what secretly lay:
Suddenly fountain's tearful flow did earn!
Alas, Alas, Alas!

Chitrangada:

With south wind in far sky,
the separated one sings alone, dear,
All buds in my garden-arbour to come out of cover, are prone.

Companions:

The one who went to woods a-hunting deer:
The poor lass, as doe, returned for lessons to learn!
Alas, Alas, Alas!

Chitrangada:

I strike at life's closed door
With anxious hands, now and before—
I haven't given up what I've in store:
in this pain, mind does shake.

Companions:

The one who had self-esteem of power
Offers basket at whose feet, with vanity to spurn!
Alas, alas, alas!

One companion:

Vow of celibacy!—
A masculine vanity it is!
At the woman's defeat,
The world's femininity would feel ashamed!
O Cupid, It's a defeat of yours!
Wake up, O God of love,

Make our companion your harbinger of victory,
Give her the weapons of the weaponless woman –
Bestow her power of defenceless maiden!

Chitrangada offers worship to Cupid and sings.

This empty basket of mine
I'll surrender at your feet.
The destitute's clothes-end, I'll
Spread as your path's cover-sheet.
Blooms with which you string flowery bow,
O Cupid, with those very flowers now, those flowers,
Let indigence of my worship's offer
Be reduced to get replete.

In your journey of war's conquest,
Me, you do take,
Flower-arrow's holy mark on my
Forehead, you make, make—
In your journey of war's conquest.
My emptiness if you do
With nectar fill,
I'll give your victory-peal
Announcing—victory-peal—
Do raise *Falgun's* call
In my and south wind's meet.

Enters Cupid.

Cupid:

O daughter of Manipur King,
Know you I do, The ascetic you!
In my worship you never had mind,
So why now so kind:

As to come to my doors?
Do tell me, you do, The ascetic you!

Chitrangada:

I had learnt a man's own skill,
To captivate mind, I never did feel—
To hold flower-bow,
In insult, my body is weakened now.
Arjuna, with vow of abstinence,
Didn't see the woman in my face hence,
Turned me down, went away.
Help me, the luckless one, I pray—
Only for one year
Flower's grace sheer:
Like heaven, let my body entail
On earth, nonpareil.

Cupid:

So I give you boon,
In your glance'll be five arrows soon,
My five arrows, soon—
They will enchant mind,
The anti-woman ascetic
Will be yours soon, too chic—
You'll make him captive in arm,
In caustic charm!
O Manipur princess,
To capture lover's heart, you'll get success.

Scene Three

Chitrangada has acquired a new beauty.

What do I behold!

Who is this in my body:
Sans past history!
Am I a dream from some by-gone birth!
I'm unknown to the world!
I'm not Chitrangada the princess!—
I'm blossomed for a single night:
In the wood, without parents any—
With only a single moment's life,
And then have the dusty bed,
Destined then for eternal neglect of earth!

She sits on the bank of the lake and sings.

Through all my limbs, who plays the flute?
In joy-sorrow, mind's stoic, absolute.

In melody of flowers' bloom,
Body-mind fill to zoom.
What sweetness and fragrance float in breeze's route!

Suddenly mind gets hope's sensation,
Fire articulates my oblation.
In my appearance and dress, I leave letter in whose address?
Words emerge from inmost heart, breaking bondage-chute.

O love-god,
Which large demon you've tied round me: as my body-companion!
What a curse it's to have this illusion of beauty! A momentary flood of youthfulness!
Entering into my blood-stream, it has maddened me!

She sings and dances in the excitement of her new grace.

In dreamy intoxication, this frenzy vain
Rouses in body-mind, what a heavy pain!
In all my veins do flow
A stream, a burning glow—
Suddenly in the whole body, a current does gain!

In stormy winds' rustle, myself I lose:
Caught in turbulent tossing youth's ruthless flood's noose.
Currents rise in soul anon
Surging in whose horizon?
There's a symbolic lingo—without words plain!

*

Chitrangada:

Forgive this one, my friend—
This one has come to deceive your eye,
Momentarily on infatuation's swing to fly
To deceive the eye.
This one descended from illusion's realm—
Carrying the key of dreams at the helm.

Exits Chitrangada.
Enters Arjuna.

Arjuna:

Whom did I behold, dear!
Is it true, or is it illusion!
Is it a physical vision,
Is it a golden ray's colourful notion!

Enters Chitrangada.

Arjuna:

Come, do come, whoever you are,
Do tell me: you're no dream, no dream either!
Ineffable graceful body: just creeper-like!

All passion's fulfillment, it does strike!

Chitrangada:

You're my guest, my own guest.
How I entertain you? Your name, suggest.

Arjuna:

I'm Arjuna, a Pandava, *Gandeeva* I hold,
O princess, behold!
Take my reputation,
Take all my action,
Take my masculine pride,
Take with whatever I abide.

Chitrangada:

(Song)

What deception this one's shape has set!
To this one, will you capitulate?
Fie, Fie, Fie!

You're brave with world-winner's vision,
This one is a woman of delusion—
Cage for this mirage: do you fabricate?
Fie, Fie, Fie!

Shame, shame, what a huge shame!
My beauty's false, false my dress's game,
It's a false dream's paradise,
Can this be your offer incarnate?
Fie, fie, fie!

Arjuna:

O the beauteous one, bestirred is my youth.
Tearing apart the monk's tie of rigid vow,
Impatience of the male virility:
I take it with pride—
I'm not like women scared by rituals,

Bound by scriptural dictate.
Come, friend, let the audacious love
Carry us along
On the way to the unknown!

Chitrangada:

Let it be then,
But do remember,
On the verge of the guilder-rose,
This little dew-drop that you see swinging—
The one whom you so ardently desire
Is the same as that droplet:
Embracing ephemera.

*

Chitrangada:

(Song)

Which god it is, wishing to tease floated boat in illusion's name,
O dream-boy, let's enjoy the heaven's curious game.
In flow of melody, in peal of laughter,
We'll float in delight in wind's rafter,
Dancing on and after,
Myrtle-wood's sweet aroma: perfumed, charmed time's lane, tame.

Unreal garland you've swung round thrilled bosom of yours:
Keep it moist in honeyed night in charm's mad water at source.
In newly-risen sun's touch of light
In shame's blow it'll have sad plight,
When day passes in new morn's sight
It'll crumble in dust, in whose shame?

Arjuna:

Today to me,
Seven heavens appear like a dream.
You're alone the complete self,
You're everything,

For lord of universe, you're a proud being.
You're an inexhaustible treasure,
One woman—you're the final end of all ignominy—
For all meditation, you're the destiny.

Chitrangada:

That me is not the real me, real me—
Alas, *Partha,* Alas!
That is an illusion of some divinity.
Go, go, go back, go back, you hero!
Valour, vigour, greatness of yours:
Don't sacrifice at falsehood's feet—
Go, go, go back.

Exits Chitrangada.

Arjuna:

What's this thirst, this burning!
This is a fiery creeper that winds round and round
The thirsty, trembling soul.
The warm heart
Seeks to burst out of all its bondage!

* * *

Arjuna sings and dances.

Turmoil has thrust on me what a scorching burn!
Cruel arrows pierced heart letting the grief run.
In bosom, fire's flames fly,
Mirage trembles in the eye,
Death's threads' welcome-garland: who has stringing done?

Known world has vanished in shady dream's vision:
In *Fagun* days' *Palash* flowers' coloured illusion.
Journey's without destination—
Missing ways is intoxication,

Going to unforeseen lands is now my turn.

Scene Four

Cupid and Chitrangada are present.

Chitrangada:

Ashes cover tired fire's action—
You'll play this game, O God, how long on?
Play of this game: when will be gone?
Whatever has to end, let smoothly end,
Dream's trace, let the graceful send.
Whatever was new: let it not be, not be worn.

Cupid:

No, no, no, friend, don't have a scare—
When flowers end their play,
Fruits have their share.
The year, oblivious of pleasure:
Let leave chant's touching measure,
Newer rhyme's pulsation.

Exits Cupid.
Arjuna and Chitrangada sing together.

Time went past on separation's mast in plucking visionary dream,
All roads at last have blended in repast in your two eyes' ream.
In eye's ream, in eye's ream.

In a trice, in whole new light
Who's created meditation's delight?
New earth, new heaven bright: have joined in our eyes' ream.

In eye's ream, in eye's ream.

Outer-sky cloud pulls up a shroud each star to conceal,
That lost glow lets its seat show: only twin eye-pairs to steal.
My wordless solitary wail
Meditated to break its spell,
Words of whole life's pain now quail: on double eye-pairs' seam.
Eye-pair's ream, eye-pair's ream.

Exeunt Arjuna and Chitrangada.
Enters Arjuna.

Arjuna:

Why does weariness come in confounded mind,
Body-mind-soul, day-night: why have exhaustion? Why so?
This debilitating mist: tear at once, leave behind,
Why keep this actionless prison in utter confusion? Why so?

Enter the villagers and sing.

Villagers:

Ho, there comes, there comes, there comes the bandits' band,
Thundering down like flood and sand—there comes, there comes.
Come you all from Panchagram,
Come you all from Kalingadham,
From Mallapalli, do land, do land.
'Victory to Chitrangada': do brothers shout—
Fear's out, fear's out, fear's out, no fears, dear.

Arjuna:

O townsmen, please do hear, please do hear,
Don't you have a saviour, dear?

Villagers:

She has gone on pilgrimage,
Taking an ascetic vow's umbrage,
She's Chitrangada, the princess.

Arjuna:

Is she a woman? And no less?

Villagers:

In affection, she's mother, in armed might, she's king, that's it.
In her name, do kettledrums beat,
'Victory, victory, victory': do brothers shout—
Fear's out, fear's out, fear's out, no fears, dear.

*

Villagers sing.

Having alarmed hesitation is self-abnegation,
Imagining obstacles: avoid a glum session.—Ah! Aha!
Get rid of fear clean,
Hold power within self: to win within.—Ah! Aha!

Protect the enfeebled one, strike at the rogue,
Thinking self as poor, helpless: should not be the vogue.
Get rid of fear clean,
Depending on self: get rid of doubt's spleen.—Ah! Aha!

When faith would blow conch, giving clarion call,
In silence, in good grace, do dedicate soul.
Get rid of fear clean,
In hard task, do prove your credentials' sheen.—Ah! Aha!

Exeunt villagers.
Enters Chitrangada.

Chitrangada:

What're you thinking, lord, what're you thinking?

Arjuna:

Chitrangada the princess
I don't know how she is,

So I wonder in mind.
I heard: in affection, she's feminine,
I heard: in bravery, she's masculine,
I heard: on throne, she's like a lion-rider.
If you know about her, beloved, do tell me.

Chitrangada:

Shame, shame, she's ugly, appearing vile.
She doesn't have such curved eye-brows,
Or such bright black eyes.

United with target can be her hardened arms,
Hero's heart can't get her eyes' oblique glances.
She has no shame, no fear, nor sense of biting humour,
With silent demeanour unmusical, her hints don't rhyme sweet.

Arjuna:

My curiosity rises a lot—
Where that brave lady can be sought?
Like a carved sword open from sheath—
Furious is she, gracious is she,
Raised thunder's awful sap is her key—
She isn't for sensuous eyes to behold;
She's the pride for the brave and the bold.

Companions:

(Song)

With woman's tempting play, why are you already weary?
Why, friend, already ended is the game?
The sweet sap that overwhelmed you:
Is it honeyed and dreary?—

Is that in dream's name?
Is that putting truth to its shame?

In absurd longing, you're filling heart,

Creating stony love-icon, you've made a start,
Wondering whatever, the manhood smart, in women, you do claim!
Is illusion, again, to blame?

Suddenly by virtue of chant
Of this soft delectation:
If our friend drops entirely notion,
Like another garb, in dirt tears it blunt,
You can't bear that disappointment—
That loud laughter which fate would vent:
We know, we know, friend, for your greedy male-ego,
It would strike a cruel arrow to lame.

Arjuna:

If I meet her, I'll rush
With her, to rescue the distressed,
From enjoyment's lure
I'll jump into battle, for sure.
Today in my fast-flowing blood
I hear the drum beat: thud--thud--thud,
Chitrangada, the princess's entity
Unites male and female identity.

Chitrangada:

How fortunate she is!
At long last her clarion call has reached your soul.
Today's new-moon night: let finally fall.
In tomorrow's pure white moon, you'll witness her,
The woman shrouded by falsity would remove her veil.

Companions address Arjuna.

Companions:

Discarding feminine tricks and gestures
To deceive men, let the woman stand up

Easy and erect, with brave strength of mind,
Like, on the hill, the fine young tree–
Let the companion of night's dalliance
Become man's colleague of action hence,
As left hand is companion of right hand,
So that, O the bravest of men, male ego be free!

Scene Five

Chitrangada and Cupid are present.

Chitrangada:

Take back, do take back
This your boon,
O Cupid lord!
Make me free, do remove
This web of falsehood
O Cupid Lord!
This pilferred wealth I'll return,
Leave it at your feet, in turn,
My body's beauty—
Red hues of these lips: let them be shun
In Ashoka wood, O Cupid Lord!

Cupid:

Let it be, then let it be,
Let coloured miasma disappear—
Let there be light: true and free.
Let illusion make way now,
Love's victory-chariot will take bow,
Beauty beyond beauty
The lover's eyes should see—

From vision, let drop this slough's greedy spree—
Let drop off, let drop off slough's greedy spree.

Exits Cupid.
Chitrangada sings and dances.

Bedecked unadorned, when will you appear –
Ornaments today: why as covers, they bear?
If love unites with illusive greed,
In light-shade, both'll lose both indeed!
When heart rushes at your easy call –
With ornaments, why covers let fall?

Whose eyes in motion's sap, always dwell,
What bejewelled glamour, to her you sell?
Having come near, why stay at far end –
In outer bondage, will you bind friend?
Your own wealth, will you yourself steal –
Using ornaments for covers: how you feel?

Scene Six

Chitrangada's companions sing, addressing Arjuna.

Come, come: the man superfine,
Come, come: the hero of mine!
The lamp is lit, looking your way.
Today from heroine's hand's end
On your glowing forehead, friend,
Wear welcome-garland gay!
She'll shatter the vanity of her power,
On your feet she'll shower self-surrender's tray—

On feet, she'll shower.

Today from heroine's hand, on your glowing forehead, friend,

Wear welcome-garland gay.

One companion:

O son of Kunti!

Because she was enamoured of you,

Our friend filled your cupped hands with bowl of beauty,

By plucking blooms from heaven's garden with much meditation.

If the worship's over, then ordain, my lord,

The offerings' basket of grace: let it lie outside temple;

Now gaze with pleasant eyes at serving maiden.

Enters Chitrangada.

Chitrangada:

I'm Chitrangada, daughter of a monarch!

I'm not a goddess, nor a petty woman!

You'll worship and keep aloft: I'm not that one, not that one;

You'll despise and push behind: I'm not that one, not that one;

If you keep me alongside in tumult and in treasure,

If you agree to my aid in hard vows in full measure,

Then you'll know me as such. I only submit today—

I'm Chitrangada, daughter of a monarch!

Arjuna:

Blessed, blessed, blessed am I!

All dance together.

Thirst's solace,

Figure of grace,

You come: remover of parting-lamentation!

Give swing to heart,

In eyes sweetly chart,

With dream's paint-brush, collyrium's vision.

Bring in mind's stance In blood's dance,

Bakul-bower's honeybees' hum-sensation!

Overflowing uproar,
On Yamuna's shore,
In tremulous bamboo-wood, wind's kiss-ostentation:
Bring on new leaves, dance-dangling chore.
Around Ashoka-branches, creepers' binding motion!

*

Come, O spring, come on earth's face—
Bring frequent notes' cascade,
Bring new life's shade,
New song's glade,
Bring idle wind bearing perfumed pride,
Bring deep consciousness in world's heart, wide,
Bring new delight's swinging motion.
Bring pleasure's rhyming movement-notion,
On earth's surface.
Come, do come.
Do break bondage of chains,
Do bring blazing soul's pains,
On earth's surface.
Come, do come.
Come with trembling tussle,
Redolent with rustle,
With honeyed aroma's delightful hustle,
In jasmine-creepers' awning, sharing with blooms' bustle,
In happy shade's retreat, in breeze sweet,
Come, do come.
Come eager to manifest,
Come with eternal zest,
Primordial wayfarer to paradise,
With flute's tune, bring union-night's rise,
Bring with you the vessel full of nectar.
Come, O the red-footed, lotus-hued, In lap of nascent morn.
Come in the moonlight-benumbed night,

Come in silent grove-cottage site,
In lake-waters sleeping in delight.
Come, do come.

Come like lightning's flare in stormy design,
In sea-water's swinging sign.
Come in morn: resoundingly awake.
Come in town-meadow-wood,
Come in chores, words and mood.
Come, do come.
Come in feet with anklets jingling,
Come in warbling voice busy singing.
Come in graceful *Mallika*-garland,
In tender shoots' dress-stand. Come in beautiful youth's speed,
Come, O exalted hero, with energy of new steed.
O the frenzied one, rush in victory's journey.
Go to the battle of victory-defeat—
Putting pollen-powder in wind,
Flying briskly hair-locks behind.
Come, do come.

*

Arjuna:

Maa mit kil tvang vanaah shaakhaang madhmateemim,
Yathaa suparnah prapatan pakshau nihanti bhumyaam,
Ebaa nihanmi te manah.

Chitrangada:

Yatheme dyaabaa prithivi sadyah paryeti Suryah,
Ebaa nihanmi te manah.

Both:

Akashau nau madhusangkaashe aneekang nau samanjanam.
Anta krinushba maang hridi man innau sahaasati.

* * *

Shyama

(The danseuse)

Scene One

Vajrasen and his friend are present.

Friend: You've crown-jewel necklace
Brought from the golden isle.
Your crown-jewel necklace—
To queen's ears, has put the case someone quite vile.
Give it to me, I'll sell to palace:
Crown-jewel necklace –
Forever, you'll be blameless.

Vajrasen: No, no, no, friend,
I've done trading quite so,
Enough give-and-take to go –
No, no, no.
For further sale isn't this necklace ---
No, no, no.
I'll swing it around someone
For whom no sale need be done –
O dear, where is she!
Till today, I don't even know.
No, no, no, friend.

Friend: Oh, don't you yet know!
Behind you, there's royal spy.

Vajrasen: I know, I know, that's why
To new land, I 'm going to fly.
This jewel I got worshipping many a divinity,
Fighting adversity—
This jewel I'll give one, searching whole city,
To new land, I'll fly.

Noticing the police-guard at a distance, friend asks Vajrasen to escape.
Enters police-guard.

Police-guard: Stop, stop—
Where do you want to flee,
Carrying quiet responsibility?
City-police spy, that's me.
Vajrasen: I'm merchant, just in case,
I'm going on own business;
In other lands, I seek to find my place.
Police-guard: What's in your chest?
Vajrasen: It has my soul, my very breath at best!
Police-guard: Open, do open, don't make vain jest.
Vajrasen: This chest is my very own rib—

Shyama, Still from Tagore Dance Film Trilogy: Shyama, Chitrangada, Chandalika by Obhi Chatterjee.

Pg 115: Shyama, Kaberi Mukherjee

Beware! beware! On it, your touch don't give!
Your or my death: then it'll spell,
If you steal it, death's name I swear to tell—
Don't touch, don't touch, don't touch!

Vajrasen flees.
Police-guard looks that side.

Police-guard: Well, well, I'll see Where you flee!
In crematorium is already planted your stake—
Remember this from now,
To your spiritual guide, take own bow!

Exits police-guard.

Scene Two

In Shyama's court, her companions are sitting, engaged in various chores.

Companions: O separated one, alas, restless is your heart—
Silently you're awake alone, in empty temple,
Keeping vigil for which missing one?
Dream incarnate, beauty peerless,
Dweller of unseen wealth-god's palace,
Whose image have you created in your suffering heart?

Enters Uttiyo.

Companions: Go back, why keep going back:
Carrying—carrying vain wish's baggage!

Forever you've kept far,
Like the unknown, in private space unfamiliar!
Come near, yet don't have passage,
Carrying vain wish's baggage!
You, we can't comprehend—
Have you got someone within,
Without search at outer end?
All your pain: unspoken and damp,
Like flame of separation's lamp,
In your eyes is lit up: what a speechless message,
Carrying vain wish's baggage!

Uttiyo: Illusive wood's dweller-doe:
Within deep dream it does go,
Why I vow to catch it now:
Makes no sense!
Let it stay on its own, far away,
Let me only on flute do play,
To touch its mind and soul, light or dense:
Makes no sense!

Companions: To dismay: don't give way, don't give way, don't give way, friend!
Unbewitched: you may stay, you may stay, you may stay,
Inside cave too dark!

Uttiyo: In *Fagun*-winds, it'd flash on sly,
In ears would enter message of sky,
Heart'll be restless now and hence:
Makes no sense!
From far, I'll make appeal,
In secret, parting-cord I'll seal,
Untied cords they are without fence:
Makes no sense!

Companions: You'll win, friend, you will win, you'll win—
Have no fear within, no fear within.

O ascetic lover, endless self-surrender is
In final outcome, stark!

Exeunt companions.
Enters Shyama with companions.

One companion: Prime moment of life don't disdain,
Don't disdain, O proud one!
Time will pass in vain, Game'll be over again—
In nectar's market, trading will be done,
O proud one!
Soul-mate, in secret, does abide, Stands by side, alas—
Walks smilingly away, floating boat in tides' vein.
Rare asset, try and get on sorrow's run:
O proud one!
When Fagun'll go away with flower-tray,
How'll you string welcome-garland, let me pray?
O proud one!
Flute'll play in distant air,
In flow of tears, in void, stare
Will pass time –
Farewell-path's footfalls in bosom will reign, in moon and sun:
O proud one!

Shyama: He's escaped so far, so far:
The one to whom I want to surrender—
Where does he hide in deep secret?
Behind each day's trifling chore: hide evermore!
Come, make my dream fulfilled,
Make my youth all too thrilled,
Make south wind in blooms' wood astir!
Do remove misery's mist,
Bring message from new life-chant.

Thirsty life's each stalled desire
Looks for words in dark quagmire –
In void, shorn of ways, in wind's rhyme,
In decayed *Bakul's* aroma sublime.

Companions practise dance, later engage in toiletry. At that time, Vajrasen enters running, followed by police-guard.

Police-guard: Catch thief, that thief, that thief!
Vajrasen: I'm not thief, that's fib, that's fib!
False blame, don't zap, Don't push me in trap—
Police-guard: That's the one, that thief, that thief!

Exeunt both.
Shyama gazes intently for a while in the direction where Vajrasen exited.

Shyama: O dear, I'll die, I'll die,
Such statuesque handsome figure, putting gods to shame!
As prisoner, whom do they bring
Like a thief in hard chains!
Go my companion, go soon, go soon—
In my name, tell the city-guard on,
Shyama is calling him.
Could he bring the prisoner just once
To my home, in good grace.

Exeunt Shyama and companions.

One companion: Bondage of the beautiful in hands of the cruel
Who can stop? Who?
Tear-flow of eyes of the hapless and the ailing:
Who can mop? Who?

Wailing of the distressed hurts universe,
Assault of injustice with poison-arrows pierce—
From assault of the mighty, who'd save weakling?
To give succour to the defamed, whose bosom'll drop?

Exits companion.
Shyama re-enters with Vajrasen and police-guard.

Shyama:	What's this grave mistake—
	Who's this god-like man you take?
	O guard, this is absurd!
	Is it fair how hard you do him tie!
	Seeing that, my spirit does die!
	You've caught him for which fault?
Police-guard:	Royal treasury has a thief's onslaught—
	We need a thief, any which way, we need a thief;
	Catch anyone, however we may, we need a thief.
	Or else we lose respect!
Shyama:	Innocent foreigner's life do protect,
	Give two days' time, have pity.
Police-guard:	I'll keep your entreaty—
	For two days, in jail he'll remain,
	Then let anything happen.
Vajrasen:	What's this game, O beauteous one!
	What's this fun?
	Disgrace-pain is done, why disgrace is done?
	Why with me why, why have such fun?
Shyama:	No, no, it's not fun,
	On my limbs, jewellery of gold
	I can give up, to accept your chains cold
	On my own body.
	At your ignominy, my own soul
	Is aggrieved as a whole.

Exits police-guard with Vajrasen.
Shyama follows for some distance and returns.

Shyama: They're king's guard, they falsely accuse
To kill the innocent in prison, under any ruse.
Please hear, please all of you hear—
Is there any hero, far or near,
Who can save him from noose of blame,
And from falsehood,
Clear his name?

Enters Uttiyo.

Uttiyo: Right or wrong: I don't know, I don't know, I don't know-
Only you I know, you I know,
O gracious one!
Do you need prime price of love?—I'll bestow,
I'll bestow, O gracious one!
Whoe'er is your lover: to save him over
My life you'll borrow—
With him ever in your bosom
I'll stay in joy and sorrow,
In death's tie,
How can you let me fly, let me fly,
O gracious one!

Shyama: So long, friend, you've sought nothing—
Sought nothing at all—
Quietly you kept eyes down overall,
Sought nothing at all.
My royal signet I do give,
My last respect, please receive.
In your hero's hand, with jewel-band,
Let my obeisance fall.

You sought nothing at all, nothing at all.

Uttiyo:

My life's vase has brimmed over with beauty you did bestow—
You haven't known, you haven't known,
You haven't known: its worth's measure how!

As tube-roses remain unseen,
Filling the night with dream's sheen and essence,
You haven't known, you haven't known,
You haven't known: in heart you did your song endow!

Time's come now to bid adieu—
Raise happy face, raise face, and raise face to view—
In sweet death, I'd give up life to fulfill my vow: at your feet.
Whom you haven't known, whom you haven't known,
whom you haven't known:
Would have his secret pain of silent night, take its final bow!

Shyama holds Uttiyo's hands and keeps gazing at him.
After a little while, she leaves his hands and exits slowly.

One companion: In the heroics of your love,
You gifted your mighty soul to our friend as a whole!
In your death's tie
Her bondage you did buy,
In sin unlimited,
In curse forever slated.
Your offering prime
Bought for our companion hell's love sublime.

Uttiyo: Guard, O guard, bind me, bind me, bind me to take away.
That foreigner isn't your accused—
Alone in guilt I stay.

Police-guard: So you've committed theft?

Uttiyo: Just see this royal signet—
Royal insignia on body I've put on today,
In that regret weep I may.

Exits police-guard with Uttiyo.

One companion: The heart is rending to pass, Alas, alas, alas!
Rare gem of youth you sacrificed, sans reason out of season, At feet of bloomless, tuneless, dusty desert to cuss, O friend!

Exits companion.
Uttiyo is in prison. Enters police-guard.

Police-guard: To gods, take a bow;
There's no more delay now,
There's no more delay now.

'Shyama', Santiniketan Asramik Shangha, Kolkata, India. *Courtesy*: Lubna Marium.

You, the wicked, Top penalty, get paid,
No end of arrogance anyhow!

Hurriedly enters Shyama.

Shyama: Do stop, do stop you all, leave him, leave him—
Guilty he is not, is not,
It's all false blame I sought,
My deception it's all—
Tie me and take me at king's feet to fall.

Police-guard: Keep quiet, go away, go away, woman—
Obstacle don't put, don't put.

Exits Shyama, covering face with two hands.
Police-guard kills Uttiyo.

One companion: What ethereal heavenly glow
Manifested, piercing annihilation-night in stormy cataclysm!
Death's grace for the terrible played the flute.
In cruel ruthless world, what did I see suddenly—
What self-surrender, with fearless smile absolute!

Scene Three

Shyama: Plays the rumbling death's own trumpets,
Storms gather far in fearful silence.
How long will I be plunged in happy dreams, forgetful of self—
Having suddenly to get up hence!

Enters Vajrasen.

O foreigner, come, do come. O beloved mine!
In mind let this word do shine—come, come—
With you in same current do float I,
Lord of heart's sky,—master of life and death!

Vajrasen: Ah, what a pleasure!
From body'n'soul, you removed all binding's measure!
Sorrow of mine is blessed today,
In depth of death comes breath of nectar's treasure!
You came to prison beyond night's season, like early dawn,
Freedom-embodied, O kind-hearted goddess of wealth!

Shyama: Don't, don't, don't call me—the kind-hearted one!
False, false, no! don't call me so!
This prison-wall has so much stone,
None's as hard as my flesh'n'bone.
I'm kind-hearted!
False, false, no! don't call me so!

Vajrasen: Do know: love's ever indebted in own joy,
Do know, my love!
Forgiving all sins is its atoning ploy,
Do know, my love!
Whatever stigma's there, It cleans and makes fair,
On dark stain, pouring nectar it does employ,
Do know, my love!

*

In love's high tide let the duo glide—bonds do unravel, do, do, do.
We'd leave despair, Back we won't stare—do set sail, do, do, do.

Tumultuous winds, waves do bring,
Heart does swing, swing, swing, swing—
O sailor crazy, Make directions hazy—do set sail, do, do, do.

One companion: Alas, O alas, alas, foreigner, Alas, homeless wayfarer!
Beckoned by blind fate,
To which unknown non-shore, you do meander?
Can you hear in distant sky
In winds, the flute of disaster?
Below coloured cloud,
Under secret tears' shroud,
God's ferocious bantering thunder?
Accumulated silent laughter?

Scene Four

Enters police-guard

Police-guard: From palace has flown the courtesan of beauty,
Where can I catch her?—it's my duty!
There's no escape, no escape from hook—
Such loss, the king won't at all brook!
From wood, why's gone the Ashoka-spike,
Making *Falgun's* court empty to strike!
Oh who're you to bewitch, her who're you to bewitch!-
Return her, let our lass have own home to reach,
Her, who're you to bewitch!

Exits police-guard.

*

Enter women. At the end, enters police-guard.

Companions: Leaving palace comfort and respect,
Our friend has come out of gate.
Don't delay, don't delay, don't delay—

How'll you go the unknown way
In dark, to find direction straight, alas!
Unknown love's sudden daze
In stormy night, has woken her gaze—in unfamiliar love!
Leaving lode-star without haze,
The friend's going towards comet, alas!
Tomorrow morning on old road
Will she be ever back to be met? alas!
Don't delay, don't delay, don't delay.

Police-guard: Stop, where do you go,
Who're you, let me know.

Companions: We're the cowherd race, Over is our sale-purchase,
To far village we dash, we're all foreigner lass!

Police-guard: Who's there sitting on the ghat?

Companions: That's our boatman-friend, smart—
We've to go quite far,
Hence we've made him stir.
Our boat he'll ply:
As boatman and stand-by.
O guard, don't stop us, don't stop us,
We plead with you, O guard!

Exeunt all.

One companion: Which cords' knots have tied two of the unknown,
In doubt's darkness grown?
Under wavy swing of side-less winds,
Union-boat'll rush beyond which parting of own?

Enter Vajrasen and Shyama.

Vajrasen: In vernal wood of hearts, the sweetness that has spread,
In love, that garland took shape, took shape, took

shape, instead.
In this bloom-necklace, beloved, I do welcome you—
Unending, sweet full of nectar: let be union-night due. Beloved, from soul-platform, in love's worship-norm, I've set cue.

*

Tell me, tell me, my dear,
You've freed me with which jewel clear?
O foreigner maiden,
To you with how much debt I remain laden?

Shyama: No, no, no—that word needn't now go!

One companion: Keep silent, my friend, keep silent,
The thorn that abides in your love,
In your bosom has it lent.
To beloved, you gave nectar,
Till today it didn't satiate hunger—
Now in it, you wish to venom be sent?
The burn that's scorching you deep within,
Why to outside, you want to vent?

Vajrasen: How did you accomplish the impossible task, tell me now!
If I know, beloved, I'll repay with this life instead,
That's my vow!

Shyama: What I've done for you, it's hard enough,
It's yet more tough: to tell you today.
The adolescent youth, Uttiyo by name,
Has been crazy in my futile love—
At my entreaty, your theft's blame he took on himself,
To sacrifice own life.

Vajrasen: You'll have to wail, O sinner, you won't get peace in life!
Den of sin will be done in—will be done in by thunder-stroke.

Shyama: O, forgive me, lord, do forgive, dear,
The curse for this sin that'll come:

Let it, in God's hand, be the more severe,
You forgive me, you forgive me, you forgive me, dear!

Vajrasen: This life's care:
It's bought at your sin's price, with that sin's share!
O disgraced one, shame of my very breath in your debt is done, O disgraced one!

Shyama: I haven't erred to you, I haven't erred.
I'm guilty to God,
His wrath'll have me debarred—quietly, that I'll clear!
If you have no mercy, I can't bear,
I can't bear, I can't bear!

Vajrasen: Won't you still leave me alone?

Shyama: I won't leave, I won't leave, I won't leave!
My sin's for you, lord, You strike in heart of your accord,
I won't leave, I won't leave, I won't leave!

Vajrasen strikes Shyama and she falls.
Exits Vajrasen.

From back-stage: Alas, what's this end!
Nectar-vessel you broke, gave it to death to rend!
This rare priceless love is lost, is lost:
In ignominy, disgrace!

Enters Vajrasen.

Village-women: Looking at you pains the mind,
Alas, wayfarer foreign,
In hot sun, on burning sands,
Have you lost road's ken?
In two eyes, what's this burn—
We don't know, we don't know: what you seek in turn?
Come, come to our abode,

Come, come for a moment's mode—
You'll get shade, get water,
Heat'll go away, peace'll reign.

*

Why doesn't he listen at all?—
Who knows where goes away his footfall?
Which messenger of death lead him to distract and disdain? Ah!

Exeunt all.
Enters Vajrasen.

Vajrasen: Come, come, come, beloved,
From death's land, bring new life's watershed.
My life's a futile lap, My world has lost its sap,
Fill empty heart with nectar in sweetness bred.

Suddenly, noticing an anklet, he picks it up.

Alas, dear, alas, O anklet!
Leaving her sad feet, you let
Sweet warble forget.
In a silent wail In pain's bonded veil you did it hold,
In separation, memory sweetly set—
Her soft feet's memory sweetly set.
At your disdainful lack of jingle, my cruel soul's beset.

Exits Vajrasen.

From back-stage: Everything why didn't take, didn't take,
Didn't take love –
Blending weal with woe.
Within himself, why didn't he forsake all embargo—

River brings in muddy water's flow,
In ocean's deep heart, it does go.
Pardon's shine gives to love's joy
A heavenly glow—
To weal and woe.

Enters Vajrasen.

Vajrasen: Come, come, come, beloved,
From death's land, bring new life's watershed.

Enters Shyama.

Shyama: I've come, dearest lover, give me pardon's cover.
Why didn't ebb, didn't ebb hard life—it does hover—
Your sad, cruel hands didn't escape give!
Do forgive!

Vajrasen: Why did you come, why come, why come back?
Go, go, go, do go away!

Shyama is leaving; Vajrasen stands in silence.
Shyama turns back once. Vajrasen advances a little –

Vajrasen: Go, go, go, do go away!

Exits Shyama, after doing obeisance to Vajrasen.

Vajrasen: I couldn't forgive at all,
Pardon my inanity, O sinner-anchor lord!
Dying in sorrow, dying in shame, life is powerless sanity—
Pardon my inanity, O sinner-anchor lord!
I couldn't draw beloved to bosom, only love I've hurt,
In order to punish sinner, I only let sin to start.

I know, dear, you'll forgive
The wretched, whom you receive under feet's magnanimity!
You won't forgive, you won't forgive
My pardon-less vanity, O sinner-anchor Lord!

* * *

Chandalika

(The Untouchable Maiden)

Scene One

A group of female flower-vendors is busy selling flowers.

Flower-vendors:

Gift-basket of new spring, we've brought to your stand!
Come, come, come:
Tie neck's garland!
Madhavi is bewailing the creepers' bondage-loss—
Into braid's bondage, do them toss.
Let them swing from swinging coiffure's band!
Come, come, come.
Wood's sweetness you can steal
New sweetness, you can instill –
Sohini melody will awaken it
In your body's vina's strand!
Come, come, come.

*

In the bunch of flowers in my garland is written
The script of spring's chanting.
In its sweetness is there an invitation of youth.
Sahana melody is coloured by its red hue,
Honeybees' hunger in unheard rhythms
Hums in their aroma.
Bring the tray, string garland gay, dear,
Bring spikes of *Madhavi-Malati-Palash* blooms.
Come you all, come you all, come you all.
Fetch oleander-*Rangan-Kanchan*-tuberoses,
Bright jasmines.
Come you all, come you all, come you all.

Put garlands on, dear beauties, put garlands on,
Make haste, dear, make haste, anon.
Today in full-moon night shines moonlight,
Bakul groves
Swing and tremble in south winds
Slowly, with soft murmurs.
Dancing wood-maidens in wood-meadows glide,
Around their mobile feet, anklets slide.
Don't let sweet night go futile, O stoic lass, alas!
Once the sacred moment's gone, it won't come again –
Nectar's jar in vain
Would go empty in the dust, *Bakul*-shoots won't last.
Installed in moonlight at night, forest-shadows with cricket-hum,
Sleepless cuckoo's parted calls in south winds plaintively come.
With myriad blooms my flower-garden has been full, dear,
Kingshuk-bunches are agitated, over them you can drool, dear!

As soon as Prakriti wants flowers, they show her contempt and exit. Enters the curd-seller.

Curd-seller: Take curd, dear, take curd, won't you now, dear?
Shyamali is my cow,
Peerless, it takes a bow!
On bank of Kankana stream,
I take her at dawn's gleam—
In verdant green-grass meadow, on river-bank's seam,
Grazing whole-time I allow, allow, dear!
Her body is black and smooth,
As I see, I like her, forsooth!
I prattle sitting nigh,
She replies with her eye,
Keeping head on my back—
On her, my hand I endow, dear!

The untouchable maiden and others come to buy curd. One of the girls cautions the curd-seller.

Don't touch her, shame, shame, don't touch,
She's untouchable, as such—
Curd'll be ruined, don't you know that much?

Exits curd-seller.
Enters bangle-seller.

O dear, each neighbourhood girl!
Come near, eyes unfurl—
I've brought bangle-pair:
Gold-wire wrap they share;
Listen to my words, put them on hand—
Whomever you want to keep, bangle'll be his shackle,
Let me tell the truth: his mind it'll tackle!

As soon as Prakriti offers hands to fit bangles—

Village-girls: Don't touch her, shame, shame, don't touch,
She's untouchable, as such!

Exeunt bangle-seller and others.

Prakriti: Whoever has sent me on to this dark ignominy,
I won't worship;
I won't offer worship any!
I won't worship.
Why should I offer, why should I offer to that god, flowers so many?—
The god who's pushed me to this shameful destiny:
Why do I, in turn, Let prayer-lamp burn

At temple-door, with longing zany!
Stealing that light,
The god put on a blight,
Keeping myself in dark uncanny!

Buddhist monks pass on the way.

Monks: *Yo sannisinno varavodhimule*
Maarasso senang mahating vijetvaa
Sambodhi maaganchhi anantayn Yanno
Lokuttamo tang pannamaami Buddhang.

Exeunt monks.
Enters Maya, mother of Prakriti.

Mother: Whatever you think in absent mind—no reason to find—
Time passes by, time passes by, dear!
In king's palace, the bell tolls there: ding dong dong, ding dong dong.

Chandalika, Darpana, Ahmedabad, India.

Pg 135: Chondalika, Shadhona, Dhaka, Bangladesh. Photo: Andrew Biraj.

Time passes by.
The sun has gone on top,
Your courtyard you didn't mop,
Water hasn't been lifted,
Fruits aren't plucked'n'sifted,
When'll let oven burn?
Take goats grazing, in turn?
Make hurry, make hurry, make hurry –
Lift water, go home, don't tarry.
In king's palace, bell tolls there: ding dong dong, ding dong dong.
There the time passes by.

Prakriti: No chores, no chores, mother,
No household chores for me!
Let them flee in flood, let all of them flee!
Why did you give me birth,
Insult in life on earth—
As mother, you brought curse prime.
Say: to whom, I did which crime?
Without sin, how unjust it can be!

Mother: Then you should lie, should lie,
In false sorrow, falsely you cry!

Exits mother. Prakriti lifts water.
Enters Ananda, Buddha's disciple.

Ananda: Give water to me, give water!
The sun is scorching, the road too long, Ha!
Give water to me.
I'm thirsty, I'm dreary,
Give water to me.
I'm weary,
Give water to me, Ha!

Give water to me.

Prakriti: Forgive, me, lord, forgive me—
I'm an untouchable maiden,
My well's water's impure;
I'm an untouchable maiden.
I don't possess the virtue:
Empowered to give you water.
I'm an untouchable maiden!

Ananda: You're the same human that I'm, maiden!
That water is pilgrim's water which satiates the thirsty,
Whatever refreshes the hot and the weary is sacred water indeed!
Give water to me, give water.

Prakirti gives water.

Blessing to you, the blessed maiden!

Exits Ananda.

Prakirti: Just a handful of water,
Ah, he took in his cupped palms like a lotus-bud,
My well became the limitless sea—
This is the dance, this is the dance of its billowy waves,
The dance that spans my life—
Oh dear, what a pleasure, what a pleasure, what huge freedom!
A handful of water—
My blemishes of multiple births have been washed away, dear, Just a handful of water!

Enter men and women.
They sing a welcome-song for harvest.

Earth has called you, do come—Oh, do come, Come, come, come!
Ripe crops have filled its bowl—so handsome, dear, so handsome!
In paddy fields with winds mad, Direction-deities seem so glad—
Sunshine's gold on earth's clothes spread its balm,
So handsome, dear, so handsome!
Listening to field's flute, sky's full of joy,
Who'd remain home any more?
Open, open the door's ploy!
Light's smile is awake in hue
On ears of corn, touched by dew,
Earth's joy brims over in waves some,
So handsome, dear, so handsome!

Prakriti: Dear, don't call me, don't call.
My distracted mind Is in some far bind—
Praying for dream to install.
Elusive shadow isn't in vision,
Bringing in mind charming illusion—
I don't know if it's divine creation,
Or it's deception tall.

I haven't lit lamp in yard's dark hood,
I'm a gardener in the burnt-out wood,
In empty hands, be a beggar, I would,
Spending day and nightfall.
If he arrives, under his feet
I'll spread my pain's sheet,
I'll tell him my tear-soaked
Wishes of empty life, small.

Chandalika, Kalamandalam, Kolkata, India.

Scene Two

The Buddhist nuns go to temple with offerings.

Buddhist nuns:

Golden-hued, resplendent, with new *Champak* bloom,
We'll worship Lord of Sages: where his lotus-feet loom.
Pious scent has filled the air, spreading its fragrance sweet,
We bring flower-garland to anoint his sacred feet.

Exeunt the nuns.

Prakriti: Blessed am I, blessed am I, on this earth: says the bloom,
O my god, your service is in my room.
I've been born in dust:
Let me forget, let me forget, let me forget, you must—
No, in heart is no dust's gloom.
Your eyes bowed-down, do make,
Petals do tremble'n'shake, tremble'n'shake.
Let me have, have feet's touch,
Dust's treasure to be heavenly as such—touch, touch, touch—
As earth's salutation, for you I zoom.

Mother: You surprise me, my girl!
I've heard in scriptures Uma made her penance In the hot sun—Is that your case?

Prakriti: Yes, mother, I've sat on meditation-platform.

Mother: For whom do you meditate?

Prakriti: The one who has given me call, given me call,
In this speechless self, words he did install!
The one who has known my name:
Oh dear, let his name in my heart stall.
Under his separation's burn,
In deep heart, I meditate in turn.

In pain's fire, let become pure
What in heart's confine does endure—
Insult-serpent's coils let fall.

Mother: What's that call, what's that call?
Which evil god from nether-worlds
Can bewitch you away?—
I'll recite chants to remove the illusion!

Prakriti: Into my mind, he has rung the words—
Give water, give water, give water!

Mother: Ah me, what hard luck!
Who told you, 'give water'?
Is he of your own caste?

Prakirti: Yes, dear mother, that's what he did say,
He belongs to my very own caste.
I'm untouchable—it's false, it's false,
It's so awfully false!
Shravan has black cloud—
If you name it 'untouchable',
Will it then lose its caste?
Will its waters become impure?
He had told me –
Don't despise yourself,
You're born in the human race,
Human blood flows through your veins.
Fie, fie, mother, don't spread false canards for self,
That'll be a sin.
In the royal clan are born numerous maids,
I'm not such a maid.
In Brahmin community are there many untouchables,
I'm not that untouchable.

Mother: What're you talking about?
Your lingo I don't follow at all!
Who has put such words in your mouth?

Has anybody possessed you in dream,
Some friend from your own last birth?
Your lingo I don't follow at all!

Prakriti: It's new birth, it's new birth, it's new birth of mine!
The other day the noon-time bell tolled, it was blazing hot sun,
I was giving bath to the orphan calf beside the well;
My Buddhist monk appeared in my front—
He said, 'Give water, give water, give water'!
My body suddenly shivered, startled was my soul—
Tell me this, mother,
Was there no water in the whole city?
Why did he come beside my well,
Why did he suddenly give me
Respect for quenching human thirst?

*

He said: give water, give water, give water!
That I can give: who's given me such succour?
He said:
give water!
Gazing at the cloud, too,
Flew in black-crested cuckoo,
It did flutter–
And said: give water, give water!
Lost in earth's dry mount
Is stream from the fount
In dark recess In prison-base.
Whose words so solemn did claim
To undo black stone's gutter—
To say: give water, give water!

Mother: Dear child, who has cast spell on you?
Your wayward mind: who has pulled it due?

Prakriti: He's my wayfarer,

Wayfarer in my heart's way.
Alas, dear! he came no more, came no more,
Came no more this way.
He didn't ask for water any longer!
My heart has become a desert thus,
It has dried up its sap—
He didn't ask, didn't ask, didn't ask for water!

*

Thirst pervades my eyes, oh dear,
Thirst fills my heart,
I'm the rainless *Baisakhi* day:
My soul gets burnt'n'hurt!
In hot winds rages the storm
Pushing mind to far void's form—
The veil goes flying apart!
The bloom that set garden alight,
Has withered now as black blight—
Fountain's impeded by whom?—
With cruel stones, tied to doom,
On sorrow's high peak's part!

Mother: Dear child, tell me in plain words:
For whom does your mind long?
Do choose a groom after your own heart—
There're are so many of your own folks.
Don't extend hand to the moon in the sky!

Prakriti: I seek him:
Who has given me the honour to serve;
The discarded thorn-apple flower:
The one who has lifted it, picking it in right hand.
O lord, O lord, Do string a garland with those blooms,
To wear round your own neck,
Don't let them waste out in vain, please don't.

Enters the follower of the palace.

Follower: Having searched in seven lands, dear,
Finally at this place,
Luckily we've met you, it's our grace!

Mother: Why dear, what's your case?

Follower: Lady queen's pet bird has flown away—
In severe grief,
She can't go to sleep, O minstrel's wife!
You've got to get it back: to give relief,
O minstrel's wife!

Mother: What's the chant that I should know to fetch a straying bird?

Follower: We won't hear, we won't hear such a false ruse—
Nor will queen listen to it: so absurd!
Use magic, recite chant to fetch it somehow,
Then we'll free you now, O minstrel's wife!

Exits follower.

Chandalika, Darpana, Ahmedabad, India.

Prakriti: O mother dear, that's the best thing.
You know your chants,
Do cast your spell to fetch him right here.

Mother: O dangerous one, what're you talking?—
It's playing with fire!
My heart trembles, I'm scared to death!

Prakriti: I'm not scared, mother, I'm not scared.
I'm only afraid, mother, lest I lose courage—
Lest I forget own worth.
Such audacity is mine: how wonderful!
He has made this wonder to happen.
Won't it happen a little more?—
Won't he snuggle to my side,
Sit in half clothes-end?

Mother: If I can bring him,
Could you pay that price?
Nothing in your life would be left any more!

Prakriti: No, nothing'll be left, nothing'll be left,
Nothing at all, nothing at all.
If everything of mine is relieved, everything relieved,
Only then I'll revive for ever,
When nothing would be left!
That I've something to gift: was the very thing
Everybody made me forget—
I've known today: I'm not the hapless one!
I'd give away, I'd give away, give away
Everything that I ever get!
I've no more fear left, as of now.
Cast your spell, cast you spell,
Bring the monk beside this disrespected one, It's she who'll give him the honour—Can anyone else give so much respect?

Mother: Dear child, you're the breast-reared gem of mine,

At your word alone, I'm the sinner going the way of sin.
O the sacred savant,
The might of my guilt
By your power of forgiveness, is far outdone.
I'd dishonour you—
Yet, my salute's to you, salute's to you, salute's to you!

Prakriti: Do blame me, do blame.
Do hold dust-laden blooms under the feet's shame.
My basket's full of guilt,
Empty yourself to get it sealed, alas,
Then in that empty bowl your mercy do claim—
You have me to blame.
You're high, I'm nil nigh, I'll entrap you
In my offence due!
Your virtues will my vice,
Above disgrace, make it rise, dear—
Stringing lapses in forgiveness, round neck, wear the same!

Mother: What a huge courage you've, my girl!

Prakriti: My courage?
His courage is peerless!
The words which none could utter
He put forth so easily—
Give water, give water, give water1
What a tiny message: with how much immense glow!
It lit up my whole birth—
The black statue that pressed on my bosom
Was pushed away—
The sap's fountain surged forth!

Mother: Who're those saffron-clad monks going along?

The group of Buddhist monks passes.

Monks: *Namo namo Buddhadivaakaraaya,*

Namo namo Gotamachandimaaya,
Namo namonanta gunannabaaya,
Namo namo Sakiyanandanaaya.

Prakriti: Mother, there he's walking ahead of all others,
There he's walking!
He didn't turn back, didn't turn back—
To look at this new creation of his own hands,
Even glancing just once!
This earth, this earth, this earth is your very own, dear!
O wretched maid, who has brought you to light
For one moment alone!
You've to be lying on earth
Under everybody's feet!

Mother: O child dear, I can't bear to see your sorrow—
I'd bring, I'd bring, I'd bring him by casting my spell!

Prakriti: Do cast your most cruel spell—
Let it coil with vicious marks to entangle his mind
Wherever he goes, he won't be able
To avoid me, to avoid me!

Mother calls her band of disciples to join in the chant of attachment.

Mother: Come you all!
Come you all!
Come you all!

Enter disciples and begin to dance.

Let him go on sea-terrain—
To return again, return again, return again. Alas!
I'll have his seat adorn On heart's throne
The road-dust in my tears I'll have lain. Alas!
Let him go to top-mountain—
To return again, return again.

Chandalika, Darpana, Ahmedabad, India.

In hill—cave I'll hide,

Call him to abide,

My dreamy face, his wakefulness, will cause refrain. Alas!

She performs an illusive dance.

Don't you worry at all—

See this magic mirror of mine—

When you dance with it in hand,

You'll see what state he is in.

Now come, come, O ferocious destroyer's son,

Create the frenzied dance anon.

Now do come on.

Scene Three

Mother dances her illusive dance.

Prakriti: See there, the clouds gather,

The spell will work, mother, will work,—
Dry meditation of the monk will fly away
Like dry leaves.
The lamp will be put out, the road will darken,
The bird from the storm-tossed nest:
It'll keep circling, to tumble down finally at my door.
My bosom trembles hard,
Lightning flashes across my mind.
Far away, the sea is gathering foam—
Sans bottom, sans shore there.

Mother: Now let me see you dance before the mirror,
Look up to observe which shadow larks.

Prakriti dances.

Prakriti: What shame! What a deep shame!
Raising his two arms towards the sky,
Whom is he giving curse?
He's hitting himself with a flaming hunter,
Piercing shrapnel in his bosom.

Mother: O dear child, if you get restive so soon,
What'll be your state at the end?

Prakriti: I won't look, I won't look,
I won't look at your mirror!
My heart's rending, O dear, heart's rending,
I won't look!
What a terrible cyclonic storm of grief—
Will the mighty forest-tree be pulled to very dust?
Will its towering glory tumble down at end?
I won't look, I won't look,
I won't look into your mirror—no, no, no!

Mother: Then let it be off, let magic be off,
Desperately I'll withdraw my spell.

Even if I lose my pulse-beats,
Even if my breathing does stop!

Prakriti: That'll be good, mother, that'll be well.
Let go your spell, do let go your spell—
There's need no more, no more, no more...
No, no, no—do cast your spell, do cast your spell—
Way left is not much more.
He'll come, he'll come, he'll come!
He'll come at the bounds of my life and death.
The wayfarer will reach in the deepest night,
In the bosom with my burn,
I'll light the lamp in turn—
He'll come, oh, he'll come!
I'll wipe your grief with my grief,
Bathe you in fathomless water of pain deep.
My family I'll let burn,
Illusive gloom'll have refining turn—
Mortal pain at your feet, as gift I'll keep.

Mother: Dear child, my spell isn't much left,
My spirit's choking my throat.

Prakriti: Mother dear, at long last I feel
As if his seat has tottered.
There he's coming, coming, coming!
What has been far away, zillions of miles away,
Beyond the sun and the moon,
There he's coming, coming, coming!—
My bosom is heaving in earth's quake.

Mother: Tell me, dear child, what do you find in the magic mirror?

Prakriti: Deep dark cloud's as if behind him,
Lightning flashes all around,
Around his limbs is the fire's enclosure—
As though it's glow of Shiva's fiery fury!
Your spell's message has spread its black serpent's hood,

Furiously breathing poison,
Polluting his sanctified flame!

Ananda's shadow-play.

Mother: O stone-hearted one, how cruel is your mind,
What a stern soul—
Still you remain alive!

Prakriti: Infatuation for him is hungry, sans mercy,
Sans fear, sans shame,
Merciless is my vow,
I won't admit defeat, won't admit defeat—
I'll bind him in illusion's tie,
I'll hug him in my laugh and cry.
Look here, he has crossed the river—
Going alone on his way in deep wood.
As if there's nothing in front of his eyes—
Neither truth, nor lies—
Neither good nor evil.

Prakriti shakes her mother.

Don't weaken, don't weaken.
Now cast your ultimate snake-spell—
The serpent-missile spell.

Mother: Not awake, not yet awake:
The hell-bound snake, not awake!
Play on play on, play on the flute,
In nether world's furious tune absolute!
Wake up the illusive-black snake: not yet awake!
Oh, to my spell lend each ear—
Pull him, pull him, pull him, clear!
Call him out in a vicious howl—

Wind on, wind on, wind to prowl!
You come out of pit,
Over seven seas, retreat!
Tie him, bring him here—
Pull him, pull him, pull him, clear!
The snake has a waking, waking, waking motion—
There's the coiling, coiling, coiling vision—
It's winding, winding, winding in illusion!
It's pulling, puling, pulling: inward notion!

*

Now in dance, you give a call—
In tune, enthrall.
Come in, join: you ascetics all!
You, come in,
You, come in,
You, come in!

All: As from deep inaccessible sleep comes up dream:
Thus you come, come!
As from *Shami* tree's trunk is ignited fire:
Thus you come, come!
As from northeast, tearing black cloud's embargo
Comes the sudden lightning,
Thus you strike a flash, to come to heart's corner,
You come, you come, do come, come!
Whereas the dark sends call in silent gesture,
As comes the Orion in evening sky,
Thus you come, you come, come!
On distant Himalayan peaks,
When chants send ascetic *Baishakh*,
Melting the hard snow-cover
As the flood's flows come streaming down—
Thus you come, you come, come!

Mother: Don't delay any further, look into mirror—

	My power is ebbing away!
Prakriti:	No, I won't look I won't look.
	I'll listen –
	Listen in my mind,
	Listen, in contemplation,
	To his fall of footsteps.
	Just look, there comes storm, comes the storm,
	Storm heralding his arrival—
	Earth is quaking violently,
	Rumbling in my bosom.
Mother:	Your curse is advancing,
	The wretched one!
Prakriti:	It's no curse, no curse,
	No curse, adverse—
	My other birth's coming,
	Death's lion-gate is opening there!—
	Breaks the gate,
	Breaks the wall,
	Breaks away this birth's falsehood!
	O my utter destruction,
	O my total possession,
	You've come on my ignominy's crest!
	Above my darkness, place
	Your own radiant feet!
Mother:	O the cruel girl,
	I can bear no more, no more, no more!
Prakriti:	O mother, O mother, O mother, do remove your spell—
	Right now, right now, right now!
	O demon, what have you done,
	What have you done—
	Why didn't you die, the vicious one!
	Where's my glowing radiance bright,
	Pure immaculate sight,

Distant heaven's light!
Alas, how pallid, how tired—
How deep the self-deception!
Leave, leave, leave,
Leave everything, leave everything—
Don't disgrace the hero,
Let victory be his—
Let victory be his, let victory be his.

Enters Ananda.

Lord, you've come to redeem me,
Such a price you've paid,
So much sorrow you've borne!
Do forgive, do forgive—
I've pulled you to earth,
Brought you down,
From dust do raise me
To your pure radiance.
Do forgive.
Victory be yours, victory be yours,
Let victory be, victory be; do forgive me.

Ananda: Blessing to you, the blessed maiden!

Everyone pays obeisance to the Buddha.

All: *Buddha susudhdhho karunaamahaannabo,*
Yochchanta suddhabbaraayanlochano,
Lokassa paapupakilesaghaatako,
Bandami Buddhang ahmaadarena tang.

* * *

Mayar Khela

(The Illusive Game)

Scene One

Forest

The illusive maidens are present.

All: We in land'n'waters in all manners, illusion's web do string.
First: We compose dreams by filling up idle eyes.
Second: Entering heart in secret, spread magic-seat's wing.
Third: We raise frenzied waves in vernal winds.
First: Distant hopes in souls commune
In cascading notes, in broken tune.
Bakul bloom loves expecting honeybees to sing.
All: We illusion's net do string!
Second: Men and women's hearts we bind in illusion-tie;
Third: How much do they keep erring, how much laugh and cry!
First: In illusion-shadow's vision, we spread in union's midst,
We bring vanity, self-dignity—
Second: To separated one in dream, union-friend we bring.
All: We illusion's net do string!

Scene Two

House

Amar is on the point of exit or exiting. Enters Shanta.

Shanta: Losing the way, you wayfarer, in the pleasure-grove—
Who do you go, where do you go?

Benumbed, bewitched, mad eyes deep in joy:
Whom do you seek, to and fro?
Where has vanished your ascetic heart, where does earth lie?
As if illusion's boat you ply, to illusion-land, slow—
Which illusion land you go?

Amar: In life, has spring come first time alive?—
Filled with new hope, what does heart aspire?
With new life, it does thrive!
In world full of joy, mind wants to rush,
Whom does it want to be seated at heart—
In searching all sides, I'll strive!

Enter illusion-maidens.

All: He's near, can't you at all see?
To look for whom, far do you flee?

Mayar Khela, Shadhona, Dhaka, Bangladesh. Photo: Ridwan Adid Rupon.

Pg 159: 'Mayar Khela', Shadhona, Dhaka, Bangladesh; *Photo:* Ridwan Adid Rupon.

Whom do you look for after your heart—
Does he on earth abide?
He's on your mind's side!
O dear, the one would be after your heart,
When you see one in pure moment's glee!
He who's your very own, him you didn't know?
Whose door will you go?
Whom you seek, you won't get,
And you'll lose mind's key!

Exeunt illusion-maidens.
Addressing Shanta–

Amar: As winds to south zoom,
Who knows where flowers bloom,
Friend, so I, too, will go—
I don't know, where I find her so!
In whose nectar-sweet voice,
World's songs rejoice,
Morn's awake in whose eye?
Whose life's loves, in infinity, dive—
Searching him on all sides, I'll strive!

Exits Amar.
Looking at off-stage—

Shanta:

Whatever my heart does seek, you're the very same, dear!
Without you in this world of mine, None else I can claim, dear!
If you don't get pleasure,
Go, go for glory's treasure—
I've placed you in my heart,
None else I need blame, dear!

I'd be down in suffering for you,
Living in your sphere,
Long days and long nights, long month and year.

If you love someone else,
And don't come back in case,
Then what you desire, you may have it,
Whatever be my sorrow-shame, dear!

Scene Three

Forest

Pramada's companions are present.

First: Friend, where's he gone? Please do him summon.
All: We'll surround him under the tree, anon.
First: In this evening sweet, In bower's blooms' midst,
He'd wander laughingly, we'll look on.
Second: In sky stars are glowing,
In south winds are blowing, From sleeping bird, tune is flowing.
First: Come, O cheerful one, bring sweet spring.
All: Under tree-creepers, grace will be grown!

Enters Pramada.

Pramada: Come, O friend, put round the neck, fancied *Bakul*-bloom garland—
Jasmine half-bloomed with care, plucked'n'groomed,
Adorn me by stringing them: to make hair-braid grand!

Mayar Khela, Dakshinee, UK.

	Pick up, dear, from forehead unkempt hair's strand.
First:	Why is such decoration? As if numb in jubilation—
Second:	Coloured lips are full of smile,
	Grace drips on earth all while!
First:	Friends, do all come and see—
	So much beauty on young body can no more land!
Second:	Prime moment of life don't disdain,
	Don't disdain, O proud one!
	Time will pass in vain,
	Game'll be over again—
	In nectar's market, trading will be done.
	Soul-mate, in secret, does abide, Stand by side—
	Walks smilingly away, floating boat in tides' vein.
	Rare asset, try and get on sorrow's run.
	When *Fagun'll* go away with flower-tray,
	How'll you string welcome-garland, let me pray?
	O proud one!

Flute'll play in distant air,
In flow of tears, in void, stare will pass time—
Farewell-path's footfalls on bosom'll be gone,
O proud one!

Third: Friend, time passed away, only games we play,
They're no more to liking,
The fervent thirst, love's long lust: why aren't in heart striking?
When would be, till life is due:
Eye-to-eye intoxicating view?—Sweet dejection, sweet heart-burn new: with daily affection hiking?
Soft liquid tears make bid to flood the eye enough,
Waters of anguish would extinguish sharp and flippant laugh.
Stoic breath would become ardent,
In hope-despair heart would rent—
Inmost thought on cheek would vent in shame's new sun-rays' dyeing.

Pramada: O dear, keep it aside, friend, keep it aside—love is a false word,
Pain of happiness, agony of caress—language is all too hard.
Blossoms' tie, fanciful cry,
Life's worship for whole life to try,
Saying 'do accept' for worship to vie—for others' feet's hope to guard.
A trifling touch'n'see to take
For years to remain pitifully awake,
For another face's smile's sake to gloat in tears absurd!
Life's pleasure put at stake for life's joy flown as bird!

Enters Amar.
Addressing Pramada—

Mayar Khela, Shadhona, Dhaka, Bangladesh. Photo: Ridwan Adid Rupon.

Amar: Don't go, don't go, don't go away,
Stand, extend feet to my heart's seat.
You're like coloured cloud in Fagun wind's sway!

Pramada: Who calls me? I never look back—
I never look back.

Amar: I seek to catch you, I never can—
Dream makes your body-span!
Don't keep me out, don't keep me out,
From your restless play!

Pramada: Who calls me? I never look back.
So many flowers bloom, Many go to doom—
I only let self flow in a pack.
My touch has joy's sap:
Leave trace, put self beyond gap,
Flowers' aroma do flow,
Creeper-leaves' breath do blow,
In woods, dejections show—
Suddenly I hear it smack—I flow in a pack.
I never look back!

Exits Amar.
Enters Ashok.

Ashok: I've come to surrender mind, I've come—
For whom my love is fulsome!
Covering mind in blossoms, leave it at the feet,
Lest they strike earth, hard—
Keep feet in heart's safeguard!
Perhaps you'll go away, pain in mind will stay—
In shore-less sea, I'm flotsome-jetsome!

Pramada: Tell him, my friend, why does he pretend?
Why false smile, friend, what tears portend?
I don't know love's flow,
So, scared I do go—
Who knows where nectar is, where venoms rend.

Companions: They don't know to cry, only make you wail—
What's false outcome: on verbal word to dwell?
Love's only a play,
Contempt all the way—
Let's return, not stay, friends, let's go as well.

Exeunt all,

Scene Four

Forest

Amar, Shanta and companion are present.

Shanta: To him, why can't I open my soul and reveal, dear?
I can't explain my heart's pain.
How does he depart with a smile,

	Have no heart to turn a while—
	Such love, such longing he insults and rolls.
Companion:	For joy, he seeks love, once without love, joy does scroll.
Shanta:	Such love full of pain none does witness,
	It remains in heart's deep recess.
	If this love were a bloom, I'd have plucked it from heart, To surrender it to his feet sole.
	Perhaps he won't lift,
	It would have to wilt,
	Still his doubt would disappear whole.

Exits Shanta.

Amar:	With own mind I do wail,
	What do I do with other's mind?
	If I can't fathom own mind well,
	How to understand mind of other's kind?
Companion:	With uncomprehending mind, you move in world,
	In soul, weeping desire's unfurled,
	If you want to give mind, do—
	Why do you long to get mind curled?
Amar:	I've known all in mind like dreams—
	'None is yours in three worlds, it seems,
	In own hope, whoever abides,
	Why do you snuggle along his sides?'
Companion:	Open eyes only to see,
	Surrender heart only on quiet plea,
	Whoever doesn't look you up,
	Let her stay in own pride hurled.
Amar:	In love if there's no joy, then why
	Is there false love, then why?
Companion:	'Give mind to gain mind's ply'—then why
	Why, dear, for moon, is there false cry?

Amar: Burning in heart flame of desire,
Illusion-mirage for eye to aspire,
In desert only to move around.

Companion: Why dear, why dear, this thirst's lie?
One who remains self-fulfilled,
In whole world has no want's yield—
There're soft winds to dwell, blooms for jewel, cuckoo-warbling bowers.

Amar: Whole universe does disappear—
How intense is love so dark, sheer
engulfing life'n'pride!

Companion: Then why, then why's this mist snide?

Pramada: I'm happy, I'm happy, friend, in my mind,

Pramada & companions: Don't desire, don't go far,
Only look around, only surround from neighbourhood.

Pramada: Friend, convey only love through eyes, silently give up heart,
Creating soft, secret verse, sing, going apart.
Quiet blooms do pluck, stringing to mark leave behind garland good,

Pramada & companions: Don't seek heart, only keep gazing only surround from neighbourhood.

Pramada: Sweet is life, sweet night's grown,
sweet south wind does blow,
Such sweetness flows on its own,
none any desire does show.
Within myself I've lost sense,
Imbued in my own fragrance—
As if my own mind, my own soul
have surrendered, I would.

Amar: Sorrow in love is a joy as well, in self, there's no joy!

Pramada & companions: No, no, no, friend, we've no illusion's ploy!
Amar: Surrender heart, do that, friend, to other's hand deploy.
Pramada & companions: No, no ,no, we have no illusion's ploy!
Amar: Joy's dew dries in a moment, sorrow's better than joy!
Bring moist'n'fresh love's own grace on lotus-leave's decoy.
Pramada & companions: No, no, no, we have no illusion's ploy!
Amar: Blooming in the sunrays, lotus drops on its own,
It gets its own happiness!
Eternal bud's life, who carries in a long dewy night, ahoy!
Pramada & companions: No, no, no, we have no illusion's ploy!

Exeunt Pramada and companions.
Re-enter Pramada and companions.

Pramada: He stands at a distance sheer,
Why doesn't he come more near?
Go you, companions, go and ask:
Those listless lips-eyes seek which jewel dear?
Companions: Fie, o fie, what's it, we'll die!
First: Who broke shame's own tie,
At long last, you're not shy!
Third: How do I go? What's to know?
First: I'll die in shame, lest he asks why?
Pramada: Go you, companions, go and ask:
Those listless lips-eyes seek which jewel dear?

Addressing Amar—

Companions: O dear, let's see, raise your eyes—

Mayar Khela, Shadhona, Dhaka, Bangladesh. Photo: Ridwan Adid Rupon.

	In your eyes, why's drowsiness?
Amar:	I've drunk something, some liquor in excess!
	In my eyes, hence drowsiness.
Companions:	Fie, fie, fie!
Amar:	friends, why to be shy?
	On earth, some're wise, some ignoramus,
	Some are conscious, some unconscious.
	In some eyes light rays pass, some eyes've tearful base,
	In my eyes, only drowsiness!
Companions:	Friend, why almost listless, standing in tree-shade hence?
Amar:	Under benumbed heart, movement, legs can't pace;
	Standing in tree-shade hence.
Companions:	Fie, fie, fie!
Amar:	Friends, what's there to be so shy?
	On earth, some stay back, some've moving process,
	Some don't wish to move in laziness,
	Some're quite free, some've feet tied in lace—
	Some've eyes in drowsiness.
Companions:	we can't make him out—come away, come away!

How does he talk, friend, what all does he say!
Come away, come away!
Not being bashful, we die in shame:
In false chore's name.
If he doesn't want to get caught, say, catch him how we may?
He only knows where his heart does stay!
Come away, come away!

Scene Five

Forest

Pramada and companions are present. Enter Ashok and Kumar.

Kumar: Friend, whatever you give of your own accord, I'll accept.

Companions: O dear, won't we die, such a sweet beggar to try!
You really want heart'n'soul!

Kumar: If you offer flowers, on head I'll set.

Companions: If you get thorns?

Kumar: Yet I'll tolerate!

Companions: O dear, won't we die, such a sweet beggar to try!
You really want heart'n'soul!

Kumar: If once you look up, friend, with sweet gaze,
Drinking your eyes' nectar, whole life I'll celebrate!

Companions: If you get a hard stare?

Kumar: By piercing heart, whole life I'll propagate!

Companions: O dear, won't we die, such a sweet beggar to try You really want heart'n'soul!

Pramada: It's not a game, not a game,
It's heart's burning flame, friend!

It's soulful impatience,
Inmost heart's painful sense—
It's pouring life and death: in whose feet's name!
As if one is calling me
Constantly with earnest plea—
'Move, move': urges soul, I can't move!
Whatever I want to say,
Perhaps not speak, I may—
Where do I bring down friend, this love's basket-frame!
Carefully stringing finally can't put, what shame!

First companion: Who's he, it's understood,
And to whom our friend set heart'n'mood!

Second and third: It's who, who, who?

First: There under that tree, With pleasure-garland free,
I don't know under which plea, what he sits to do!

Second: Friend, what'll happen—
Will he ever come near, will he speak then?

Third: Does he know love? Does he bondage serve?
In which Illusive way, he's caught mind, too!

Second: With confused eyes, at eyes he does gaze,
As if he came, losing way in a haze, O dear!

Third: As if in singing voice His ears do rejoice,
As if in some moonlight, he's rapt and does coo!

Pramada: Friend, everyday goes back who?
To him give a bloom from my hair, you do,
If he asks from which flower-orchard,
On my oath, don't give my name, too!

Companions: Then, how'll you catch him, friend, if he does get caught?

First: How will you make him cry, if your own crying you wrought!

Second: If you want to receive heart, keep heart in secret!

Third:	Who'll tie him down, if own tying you sought!

Amar comes near Pramada, addressing her—

Amar:	Whole-heartedly whom I loved Me, could he return, friend? I'm outside earthly life, I don't know what happens here, in turn. Who knows, if soul seeks desperately a soul, It gets or not, on the whole—I don't know. To unknown heart's door, so in fear, I've run. I love your everything—all that grace, That game, that song, laughing sweet face. With that you envelope life of mine— Where's your boundary in whole world's sojourn?
Companions:	Who're you, why to friend your desire convey?
Second:	Who wants to know if you love or not, what all you want to say.
First:	Smiles the moon, smiles evening, bower-wood has pleasure— Full youth smiles in heart's spring in full measure. Why don't you smile, why heave sighs, to burn?
All:	Have you come for games to end— Stop hearts' fete: friend to friend?
Second:	Own sorrow, own shadow: take away; To life's pleasure-path: give way!
Third:	To worship the lotus-seated, from far you learn.
Amar:	Then be happy, be happy, let me go—go.
Pramada:	Friend, call him back, to false games say no.
Companions:	Don't be too eager, friend, For fulfilled hope none returns, for unfilled hope one does beg!
Amar:	I was alone in my world—where's this I've come?

I don't know the way, let me return,
If that rest-house I get back, in turn.

Exits Amar.

Pramada: Friend, call him back; to false game, to false shame: say no.

Companions: Don't be too eager, friend,
For fulfilled hope none returns, unfilled hope one does beg!

Exeunt all.

Scene Six

Amar and Shanta are present.

Amar: My whole world has been lost,
Universe's *vina*-tune has come to die.
Homeless heart does pass to unlit way, alas!
On deep dark cave-floor, I go down to lie!
In your eyes is the even-star's light,
Upon my way's dark, let it shine bright.
Going behind mirage again,
Thirsty hours've passed in vain.
At day's end in your heart,
Restive, nectar-pilgrim wayfarers ply.

Shanta: Don't you err, don't you err,
Don't you err in love.
Don't mislead, don't mislead, mislead with vain hope's dove.

I stay with parting's pain,
It doesn't evade me in vain—
His lingo I know to serve.
With hoax kindness, don't be cruel,
Seeking to give heart, don't break heart's jewel.
Don't keep charmed—
In death's flute, embalmed,
Don't drag into danger's cove.

Amar: I had erred, mistake is gone.
I am awake, I've known—no more mistake, no mistake.
Behind illusion,
I've moved, I've known dreams to be false—
Thorn has pricked soul—it's not bloom's sake, not bloom's sake.
Love I won't neglect,
With hearts, I won't play-act—I won't play-act.
In your heart, friend, I seek refuge.
In shore-less sea of life—there's no shore to take, no shore to take.

Enter companions of Pramada.
From afar—

Companions: Bees go many times away, bees many times return—
Then flowers bloom, in turn.

Pramada: Buds want to bloom, don't bloom—die in shame, in heartburn.
Forgetting pride-insult, yield mind'n'heart, for always intimate sojourn.

Second: O dear, giving up hope, still keep hope, for heart's jewel to earn.

All: Come back, do come back—wood's aroma to adjourn.
Today's separation night, bloomed flowers dew-

waters churn.

Amar: Don't call me, don't call, don't call,
He who has come away, in mind don't recall.
I've taken away my own anguish,
Having loved, I didn't ask for a niche,
With a grain of pity in side-long glance, don't enthrall.
Current of high-tide of all my sorrow
Away from all disgrace, would push me to morrow.
When I go far away,
Then recognise me, you may—
Today in neglect and deceit, don't you stall.

Addressing Amar—

Shanta: Without comprehension, whom do you, in tears, let flow?
O dear, who keeps looking at the void—
Who has no joy in life, whose heart does flow?
You haven't read whose eyes' word?
Whose inner hope, you haven't heard,
You didn't look back—
Whose eager heart's desire, you let blow?

Amar: She who did roam in my dream
Was incomprehensible, it would seem;
Days went by in constant quest.
In auspicious moment you called,
My immodesty you stalled, dear,
You're one whom I understood best.
Who would return me in neglect?
Who would call me with care?
In whose pain of love, my value I do share?
This perennial doubt, alas, I cannot beset,
You alone I've understood best.

Exits Amar.

Shanta: O wretched one,
In currents, boat floated away, to coast, it didn't turn, didn't turn.
You spent time in stringing *vina's* tune—
In hard pull, it didn't commune,
In broken chords, melody couldn't run.
Coming beside this road,
It called you overboard.
You've turned him away, closing your bay—
Heart was burning, yet forgiveness, why didn't I learn?

Scene Seven

Forest

Amar, Shanta, and other townsmen and women are present.

Women: Come, come, spring, on earth's face,
Bring your notes, love's song.
Bring idle wind redolent with aroma's intoxication.
Bring new youth's melody, new life along—
Pleasant, nascent longings on earth's face.

Men: Come with trembling, shuddering rustling voice,
New leaves to rejoice.
In jasmine creeper's groves: restless with flowers—
In shades joyous
Breeze gracious
Come, come.
Come with red feet,
With lotus replete: in new morn's lap.

Come in night, numb in moonlight, in rumbling noise of river-water coast,
In placid lakes that happily slumber, come, come!

Women: Come in youth-affected heart,
Come in eyes idling in union's joy,
Come within sweet shame—inter-locking arms with arms.
In new flower-ties, create nascent union's bond.

Enter Pramada and her companions.

Amar: Is it dream! Is it illusion!
Is it Pramada! Or her shadowy vision!
Did she come, or didn't she?—

Men: It could, or couldn't be!—
Was it illusion, or dream's shadow vision—or magic to see?

Amar: Does she get caught in beauty's cord?
Can music-notes tie her of own accord?
She's eternal separation's plea!

Shanta: In his flute there's sad tune
Blending union-separation to commune.
In weal or woe, getting, not getting,
In heart's wood, his stoic wind is setting—
Perhaps he's deep desire's key!

Amar: Is it dream! Is it illusion!
Is it Pramada! Or her shadowy vision!

Companions: Which storm's erring zoom Let it drop the bloom,
As its first young sweetness made the bud to loom!
The early morning star
In evening, lost its way too far.
In gods' abode for heavenly maidens it was earrings' plume!
It's crown-beauty's show—
If you do get one too compassionate, on head, let touch go.
Will currents' strand carry it to far cruel land—

	I don't know, at day's end, which shore it'll assume!
Shanta:	Fie, fie, I die in shame,
	Who adorned me falsely in decoration's name!
	In God's humour sly,
	Quietly I've been here to try
	And come between you two, I may;
	I'm not there, not there in grace—
	Adored one, do take your place,
	Where your seat do stay.
Shanta and women:	In pious union moment, let flute play,
	In cloudless sky, let smiles be gay.
Men:	In much sorrow, from too far,
	Roaming around dark seas astir,
	The golden boat has come to shore.
	O city-maids, you please may bring decorated reception-tray,
	In duo's union's big festivity
	In conch-sound's gaiety,
	Spring's pleasures do tumble galore!
Pramada:	No more, no more!
	Why does spring-breeze carry more dry blooms' chore!
	The moment has gone,
	All hopes are forlorn—
	Which lamp you've lit, it burns my bosom sore!
	My orchard has been a desert—
	Today in evening darkness
	Which flowers do you pluck apart!
	From whose fate, reception-tray you steal—
	Broken basket to conceal.
	Union-garland's baggage of thorn
	How tolerantly the neck bore!
Amar:	Carrying broken chain, O bird,

Fly away, fly away: alone, absurd!
The bond on your feet should lay,
In wings, you'll get joy gay!
Confounded clouds called galore!
In clean sorrow freedom exists, in clean void's love,
Self-deception is a big shame, thoroughly spent, let it serve!
In life-death's unrealisable longing,
So far, you were in cage's belonging—
You'll be laid in dusts' score.

Shanta: Falsehood's web: let it be torn, let it be torn!
As bounty of sorrow, today freedom is born.
This is well, dear, this is well—Let separation-fire's flames dwell.
Cruel truth bestow the boon—deception's hiding let be shorn!
Go, beloved, do go in victory-chariot!
On way, I won't put blind spot,
Before you farewell, do take,
Your mind from dream should be awake,
Let all hubris be cleansed this morn!

Illusion-maidens: From sorrow's sacrificial fire, the love that flows
Like gold, it glows—
It's enduringly free from doubt, Glory is its undying clout!
Beyond unrealisable longing
In separation's holy place, it does abide,
Where burns restless sacred pyre's eternal despair snide:
Free of burning thirst
It's always spotless without doubt,
In water-bath from tear's fount,
It's immortal ascetic about!

Exeunt illusion-maidens.

All: Today come to play the termination of all play, come!
You'll break the happy home of clay, come!
Union's garland'll break its tie,
Fagun day's dream today will die—
Missing mind's wings you'll lay, come!
On sun-set hill, the peak's in the sky:
Banners of stormy clouds today fly.
There'll be dance of nor'wester—
Get your life-death dance faster and faster
Laugh'n'cry under feet you'll slay, come!

* * *

Glossary

Arka	The sun
Ashok	A kind of flower tree
Baishakh	Bengali summer month: mid-April to mid-May
Baishakhi	Related to Baishakh
Bakul	Large ever-green flower tree
Chandali	Untouchable maiden
Fagun, Falgun	Bengali spring month: mid-February to mid-March
Kanchan	Golden flower
Kingshuk	Beautiful red flower
Madhavi	Evergreen creeper
Malati	A kind of Jasmine
Palash	Beautiful red flower
Piyal	A kind of nut-tree
Prakriti	Nature as female force
Purusha	Male force behind universe
Rangan	A kind of red flower
Sahana	Indian classical musical mode
Shami	A kind of large tree
Shravan	Bengali rainy month: mid-July to mid-August
Sohini	Indian classical musical mode

* * *

Dr Utpal K Banerjee has been an adviser on Management and Information Technology for thirty-five years, after having studied on a doctoral programme in the UK as a Commonwealth Scholar from 1968–1972. He has an abiding interest in Indian art and culture. His formal exposure to the visual and performing arts of the world was through courses conducted at the Extra-Mural Department, University of Manchester, UK. He has been National Project Director for the Indira Gandhi National Centre for the Arts (IGNCA) relating to the UNDP project on Multimedia Database for Art and Culture Documentation and Computerisation from 1991–1993.

In the nineties, Dr Banerjee gave lectures on Indian art and culture, organised by the Indian Council for Cultural Relations (ICCR), in Canada and South America. He was also invited by the Kala Bharati Foundation of Canada to speak on the same subject.

He has been writing on the arts and culture in several newspapers and journals and is a regular contributor on cultural and professional programmes to London BBC, All India Radio and Indian television. He has also written 33 books, including *Hindu Joy of Life* (Niyogi Books, Delhi, 2006), which has gone into a second edition.

Dr Banerjee was awarded the Padma Shri 'in recognition of distinguished service in literature and education' in 2009.

His recent Tagore studies include *Tagore's Mystique of Dance, Tagore-nama, Mystic Songs of Tagore* and four volumes of *Rainbow Rhymes of Tagore* under: *Humour & satire, Mother & Child, Wish Fulfillment Foray* and *Fantasy Poetry*.